TUDOR DRAMA
AND
RELIGIOUS CONTROVERSY

TUDOR DRAMA
AND
RELIGIOUS CONTROVERSY

by

James C. Bryant

MERCER

ISBN 0-86554-129-9

Tudor Drama and Religious Controversy
Copyright ©1984
Mercer University Press
All rights reserved
Printed in the United States of America

Library of Congress Cataloging in Publication Data
Bryant, James C.
    Tudor drama and religious controversy.

    Includes index.
    1. English drama—Early modern and Elizabethan, 1500-
1600—History and criticism.   2. Religion and literature.
3. Church and state—England—History—16th century.
4. England—Church history—16th century.   I. Title.
PR658.R43B7   1984   822'.3'09382   84-10850
ISBN 0-86554-129-9

CONTENTS

DEDICATION

TO PROFESSOR THOMAS B. STROUP
Mentor and Friend

INTRODUCTION

When the Spanish ambassador, de Quadra, reportedly announced that during Elizabeth's reign religion in England had become merely a matter of politics, he was simply articulating a point necessary for our understanding much of Tudor history and art. From our modern perspective, accustomed as we have been to the principle of separation of church and state in Britain and America, it is easy to minimize the importance of the Roman Catholic and Protestant struggles for supremacy throughout the English Renaissance. That is, it becomes convenient for us to dismiss recurring allusions to religious controversy in contemporary literary documents as simply problems in church polity or, at most, merely questions of religion that were not really part of the mainstream of English affairs. However, nothing could be more inaccurate.

Religious questions were so much a part of the Englishman's practical, everyday life that his fortune, reputation, and sometimes even his life depended upon which side of the religious disputes he chose. Certainly in England the struggle could never be called merely religious in the sense that modern men are apt to understand that word. Actually, Tudor religion was often inseparable from politics.

The drama of the period largely reflects issues of religious controversy that were to decide the destiny of England either as an independent nation, whose kings ruled by the grace of God, or as a temporal fief of the See of Rome, ruled by the grace of the pope. It was an issue that was contested not only in theological and political tractates but in consistory courts, heresy purges, Smithfield fires, beheadings and hangings, a

Spanish invasion, and frequent attempts to assassinate the queen. All of these physical manifestations of the controversy between the papacy and the English kings provided dramatists of the age with materials for use in stage plays—both as propaganda and as entertainment.

It is helpful to remember that Tudor dramatists wrote for a popular audience; that is, they held up the mirror to reflect both nature and the times in which they wrote. They did not necessarily prescribe public taste; they echoed it. They recognized materials for their stage plays in the bitter religious disputes.

One of the recurring themes in dramatizing historical struggles was the alleged usurpation by the Roman pontiff of ancient liberties claimed by English kings. Frequently playwrights used this theme to appeal to the popular sentiments, fears, and natural suspicions of a highly patriotic audience. There it became little more than propaganda in support of the governmental policies that restricted the settlement of ecclesiastical affairs to within England. At other times the vitriolics may have been toned down considerably, but the dominant point of view was still a sanction of the English Reformation directed toward a popular audience. Thus, when Marlowe's Edward II asks the question "Why should a king be subject to a priest?" it is really a topical allusion to a question reaching back through several centuries of ecclesiastical controversy—at least as far back as the time of William the Conqueror.

Before one can place a question such as the one posed by Marlowe's Edward II in proper perspective, it is necessary to become aware of the political and religious issues leading up to Henry VIII's reformation of the Church of England and to observe Rome's persistent endeavors to reclaim the English Church from her solitary course at any cost. Tudor dramatists often gleaned their material from the annals of Church history. Without some frame of reference to the English royal prerogatives and the rival papal claims upon the island nation, much of the religious controversy in the dramatic literature of the period becomes meaningless.

CHAPTER I

PRE-TUDOR
CONTROVERSIES
WITH ROME

As far back as the coming of William the Conqueror to the throne of
England there appeared a breach between church and state that
could never mend. It was destined to result in Henry VIII's reformation
of the Church in England.

The first hint of separation was perhaps too slight to warrant much
notice from any observer at the time. But looking backward, one sees the
issue in focus as William separates temporal and spiritual administration in England. William was willing to appeal to ancient prerogatives
traditionally claimed by British kings when it suited his purpose, especially in matters of lay investiture and providing benefices for the
Church. But when he separated jurisdiction into ecclesiastical and secular law courts, he opened the door for what would eventually become
absolute dependence upon spiritual as opposed to temporal powers. As
a result, weaker successors to William would soon be forced to submit
to both the temporal and spiritual jurisdiction of the Roman See for their
very right to ascend the throne of England.

Yet William's own keen sense of administration allowed him to draw
a fine distinction between matters he considered spiritual, therefore sub-

ject to the papacy, and matters temporal or political, therefore beyond the jurisdiction of the Roman See. Later, Henry VIII made a case for his separation from Rome largely upon this same base.

While the Conqueror was imposing his own reformation upon the Church in England, particularly in denying the right to have questions involving canon law or spiritual offenses tried before ancient courts of the land, the very powerful Pope Gregory VII (Hildebrand, 1073-1085) was busy with his own version of church reform. Hildebrand's great objective seems to have been the complete subjection of all civil powers to the ecclesiastical. Moreover, his interpretation of the clerical office was that it should be a separate and distinct order, not bound by citizenship to any temporal state. But two such formidable, opposing powers as William the Conqueror and Pope Gregory VII were eventually bound to engage in controversy over their respective claims of administration.

The first evidence of religious controversy between the two became apparent in William's letter to Pope Gregory, written about 1076.

> Hubert, your legate, Holy Father, coming to me in your behalf, bade me do fealty to you and your successors, and to think better in the matter of the money which my predecessors were wont to send to the Roman Church: the one point I agreed to, the other I did not agree to. I refused to do fealty, nor will I, because neither have I promised it, nor do I find that my predecessors did it to your predecessors. . . . Pray for us, and for the good of our realm, for we have loved your predecessors and desire to love you sincerely, and to hear you obediently before all.[1]

All of the seeds of the recurrent religious controversy up until the English Reformation are contained in the Conqueror's letter. King William recognized the spiritual authority of the papacy and was willing to send the Peter's pence to Rome. But, as king of England, he refused to acknowledge the pope's temporal authority over him. Moreover, he based his refusal upon the grounds of English royal precedent. Many aspects of the controversy until Henry VIII's quarrel with Rome are merely variations on this theme.

King William's assertion of supremacy over ecclesiastical matters within his dominions was but an extended appeal to ancient royal precedent in England. He, much like Edward the Confessor, functioned

---

[1]Henry Gee and William John Hardy, *Documents Illustrative of English Church History* (London: Macmillan and Company, 1910) 56.

both as Defender of the Faith and as Supreme Governor of the Church in England—a fact that takes the edge away from Henry VIII's claim. It is also clear evidence of the point that religion and politics were inseparable in English ecclesiastical administration from the beginning of her national consciousness.

When Stephen became king in 1135, Pope Innocent II wrote him a letter acknowledging his election by popular consent and formal consecration. At face value the letter seemed harmless enough to the temporal rights of the king, but Stephen turned it to other uses. Actually the matter of the king's relationship with Rome had been settled before his coronation. Upon Stephen's accession, the bishops of England took an oath of loyalty to their king on the condition that he agree to preserve the liberties of the Holy Church.

The issue was clear when Stephen signed his famous charter containing the following important paragraph:

> I, Stephen, by the grace of God and the assent of the clergy and people elected king of the English, and consecrated by William, Archbishop of Canterbury and legate of the Holy Roman Church, and confirmed by Innocent, pontiff of the Holy Roman See, from regard and love to God, do grant holy Church to be free and confirm due reverence to her. . . . I permit and confirm justice and power over ecclesiastical persons and all clerks and their effects, and the distribution of ecclesiastical goods to be in the hands of the bishops.[2]

Of critical value is the manner in which Stephen conceded to the pontiff what no English king before him had ever conceded—his right to rule as being contingent upon the confirmation of the bishop of Rome. From the time of this single concession by Stephen it would be a mere eighty years before the English Crown became a vassal of the pope. Stephen's concession opened Pandora's box in the realm, and no amount of theorizing could control the innovations from Rome which followed. The end result was toward the same goal—the transferring of ecclesiastical power out of England and into the hands of the bishop of Rome.

The long religious dispute between the papacy and the English kings seems to have been settled in favor of Rome. Stephen made a bid for papal support in order to secure his rule, but in doing so he lost the right

---

[2]Gee and Hardy, 66.

to rule according to ancient customs in England. Henry II fought manfully against what he saw as foreign encroachment upon royal prerogatives. Although his Clarendon Constitutions were in a sense merely the codification of laws and customs dating back to the days of Edward the Confessor, such attempted legislation on Henry II's part was unfruitful. It would take a Henry more powerful than Henry II to restrain papal encroachment on the English nation.

The troublesome reign of King John (1199-1216), which later supplied Tudor dramatists with effective materials drawn from the religious dispute in support of the English Reformation,[3] was a critical turning point in the controversy with Rome. King John had fallen out with Pope Innocent III in 1205 over the election of the archbishop of Canterbury. When that office became vacant, the canons composing the cathedral chapter at Canterbury elected one of their own members without first consulting the king. Still in violation of royal statutes, the canons sent their archbishop-elect to Rome for confirmation. When John discovered their intention, he proposed his own candidate and also sent him to Rome for confirmation.

Pope Innocent heard both sides and declared in favor of neither candidate. Instead, he proposed Cardinal Stephen Langton, an Englishman trained in papal service. Although the canons were willing to accept the pope's decision, King John swore in anger that he would not allow the pope's man to enter the kingdom. As an added measure, he would keep the archbishopric vacant. Pope Innocent retaliated by issuing his famous interdict upon England in 1208, releasing John's subjects from all oaths of loyalty.

Not to be outdone, John seized all church properties in England and compelled the clergy to recognize royal supremacy. Despite excommunication, the king continued his stubborn defiance of Rome's demands for the next five years. At last, in 1212, Pope Innocent declared John deposed, and to effect the deposition he ordered a crusade against England by a French invasion. It was not until John's rebellious barons refused to fight for him—even in the face of a French invasion—that he submit-

---

[3]Specifically, it inspired John Bale's *King John* (c. 1538), the anonymous *Troublesome Raign of John, King of England* (1591), and Shakespeare's *The Life and Death of King John*.

ted. Thenceforth, following the example of King John, kings in England were expected to hold their dominions as papal fiefs.

By 1295 war had broken out between France and England, and King Edward I summoned Parliament to meet the crisis. No doubt Edward wanted money to finance his military campaign more than he wanted counsel, and it was from the clergy that he expected the needed revenue. But the clergy surprised him by appealing to Rome for intercession against the king's taxation.

Pope Boniface VIII (1294-1303) responded to the appeal by issuing his bull *Clericis Laicos* (1296). It was designed to stop Edward I from financing his war effort by ecclesiastical taxation, but Boniface also used the occasion to air other grievances against Edward. Laymen, he pointed out, had been hostile to clerks from antiquity. Some people did not "consider how power over clerks or ecclesiastical persons [was] forbidden them"; some "impose[d] heavy burdens on their prelates"; "and in many ways they essay[ed] to bring them under slavery and subject them to their authority." The hostility had reached the point, according to Boniface, at which prelates and other ecclesiastics were "alarmed where there should be no alarm" and were "seeking transient peace, fearing more to offend the temporal majesty than the eternal." The pontiff then declared that any ecclesiastics who should further acquiesce by paying such taxes, and any laymen who should exact such payments from the clergy, would be excommunicated.

Thus fortified by the threat of excommunication, the English clergy refused Edward's demands for payment. But the king, equally determined, outlawed the clergy and seized the properties of Canterbury. When a similar situation was developing in France, Boniface modified his position. The announcement came from Archbishop Winchelsey: the pope would extract financial aid from the English clergy if the king would agree to restore Church liberties. Pope Boniface explained that his bull did not forbid voluntary financial aid from the clergy, and if absolutely necessary, the English king could extract taxes from them. In this phase of controversy with Rome, Edward I won a clear victory.[4]

---

[4]George Peele's *Edward I* (c. 1593) has the significant parts of Edward's reign as its base. In the last act, Queen Elinor, who is on her deathbed, confesses to her husband (disguised as a friar) that her child, supposedly by the king, was actually begotten by a Roman Catholic friar.

Meanwhile, Edward was moving toward another dispute with Boniface over the jurisdiction of royal overlordship in Scotland. As an invited arbiter in the succession to the Crown, Edward decided in favor of John Balliol, who thus acknowledged himself as a vassal of the English king. But when Edward ordered him to enter the war against France on the side of the English, Balliol refused. Edward then deposed the Scottish king and administered his own government there, even defeating the celebrated William Wallace.

Pope Boniface entered the controversy by issuing a bull in 1299 claiming Scotland as a fief of the papal see and ordering Edward to cease hostilities against the Scots. But Edward, having learned the necessity for administration through representative assembly, answered that such a demand from the pontiff could be decided only by Parliament.

Parliament met at Lincoln, and the barons prepared a statement in reply to the pope's demands in which they declared that upon hearing the pontiff's claims, the baronage found the matter "astonishing" and "unheard of." For, they explained, from the days of England's first founding, the English "have had the superior and direct overlordship of the realm of Scotland." In fact, they continued, all kings of England had acknowledged that Scotland was their fief, just as the Scots and their kings had never been "subordinate nor wont to be subject to others, but the kings of England."

Parliament unanimously replied to the pope that Edward "shall in no wise answer judicially before you, nor undergo judgment in any matter whatsoever, nor bring into doubtful questioning his rights aforesaid"; to have done so would have been a violation of royal prerogatives, customs, and paternal laws to which the barons were committed by sacred oath. Furthermore, to obey the pontiff in this demand would have, according to the barons, "manifestly tend[ed] to the disherison of the right of the crown of the kingdom of England, and of the royal dignity, and the notorious subversion of the estate of the same kingdom." Therefore, Parliament would not permit the king, "even if he should wish it," to obey the pope's demands in this matter.[5] The document was signed by one hundred and four barons of the realm. This maneuver was one of the

---

[5]See the Barons' "Letter to the Pope," in Gee and Hardy, 89-91.

boldest acts of defiance by a collective representation of the English nation against papal encroachment in temporal affairs to that date.

Such an act of defiance of papal claims, combined with a similar act of defiance by Philip IV's *États Généreaux* in France (1303), was a direct affront to Pope Boniface's projected image of himself as virtual "dictator of Europe" at the great Jubilee at Rome in 1300. He had issued his famous bull *Unam Sanctam* in 1302, the most presumptuous claim over temporal states ever made by a bishop of Rome. Apart from its declaration that obedience to the bishop of Rome was necessary for one's salvation, *Unam Sanctam* presumptuously announced papal claim over all the temporal states of Europe without exception or equivocation. But the bull found stiff opposition both in England and in France. France, for example, retaliated by accusing Boniface of many crimes and by ordering his trial before an ecumenical council. After the pope's arrest at Anagni, his palace plundered and his life threatened, Boniface was released and allowed to return to Rome. He died a month later.

If anything positive came from the pope's humiliation, it was a sentiment of national consciousness which surged in both England and France. Neither country was willing to relinquish all temporal authority to what it considered essentially a spiritual office. In England, as a matter of fact, a patriotic nationalism became the ultimate weapon against which Rome was held in check on her side of the ecclesiastical controversy. From the time of Pope Boniface's humiliation, Rome's design for absolute world domination in temporal realms became an impossibility. The English Reformation under Henry VIII was but a matter of time. The reestablishment of royal supremacy in England was won bit by bit over the next two centuries.

A clue to the changing climate was apparent during the reign of Edward II (1307-1327).[6] During that weakling king's reign, the papacy was set up at Avignon, but Pope Clement V (1305-1314) was himself by birth a subject of the English Crown. In an effort to restore better relations with the temporal power, Clement could say that he had never appointed an ecclesiastic to a benefice who was not a subject of the English king in either England or his dominions across the channel.

---

[6]The career of Edward II provided Christopher Marlowe with materials for effective drama in *The Tragedy of Edward the Second* (c. 1592).

Another step toward restoring royal prerogatives in England was taken by Edward III (1327-1377).[7] It dealt with the touchy problem of papal provisions. Despite the continual controversy as to who should dispose of vacant benefices, pope or king, the issue was never settled to the satisfaction of all parties. For example, whenever vacancies were not clearly decided through normal procedures of cathedral chapters, both king and pope claimed jurisdiction; the king claimed it as "regalian right," and the pope claimed it as his own right of provision.

Parliament expressed the sentiment in England against Rome's claim by enacting the Statute of Provisors in 1351. That statute made reference to other legislation, such as the Parliamentary Act at Carlisle (1307) against papal patronage and the forbidding of goods and money being sent out of the realm from religious houses to their foreign superiors. By the Provisors Act all papal provisions were declared illegal and punishable by royal courts. Moreover, the right of provision was returned to the king's jurisdiction where it had been before the papacy claimed that right.

In order for ecclesiastics to obey the king in England, legislation was required to prevent their being summoned to the papal court and ordered to comply with the pontiff's wishes in the matter of provisions. Parliament met at Westminster in 1353 and passed the first Statute of Praemunire, which forbade cases claimed by royal jurisdiction from being carried out of the realm for settlement by the Roman Curia. In fact, Praemunire declared it treason to appeal to Rome against the king's decision: the offender was to be outlawed and his properties forfeited. It was, however, not so much an attack upon the pope as it was an endeavor to keep Rome from claiming areas that English kings had traditionally claimed by royal precedent.[8]

Another phase of the religious dispute between England and Rome became apparent during the reign of Richard II (1377-1399) concerning the matter of John Wyclif. Almost a year before the Great Schism, Pope Gregory XI (1370-1378) in vain sent a letter to Archbishop Sudbury and

---

[7]The career of Edward III forms the basis for the anonymous Elizabethan drama entitled *The Reign of King Edward III*, written sometime during the years 1592-1595.

[8]For additional consideration of Praemunire, see W. T. Waugh, "The Great Statute of Praemunire 1393," *EHR* 37 (April 1922): 173-205.

the bishop of London ordering proceedings against Wyclif (1324-1384). Although the letter was merely one of the five papal bulls issued by Gregory XI against Wyclif, it represented the whole complaint of the Roman Curia against the Oxford don turned reformer.

Pope Gregory began his letter by pointing out that England, once so "glorious for the piety of faith, and radiant for its renown in the sacred page," had been distinguished in former days for "champions of the orthodox faith," holy learning, and sacred influence. Now, however, "enemies enter into it to prey on the most precious treasure of men's souls." Although the English prelates near at hand were reluctant to resist the enemy, the "sly entries and open attacks [were] noted in Rome." He was, of course, referring to the fact that Wyclif seemed to propagate his ideas in England unimpeded. Gregory continued to admonish the prelate and bishops for negligence. He ordered Wyclif arrested and a confession to be extracted from him. Moreover, he ordered that Wyclif be kept in prison without benefit of appeal. The secular arm, if need be, should be called in to keep Wyclif in custody.[9]

Another letter from Gregory stated that if Wyclif could not be arrested, a public notice should be posted at Oxford and at other places summoning him to appear at the papal court within three months to receive due sentence. Still another letter directed the prelate to warn the royal family, nobles, and counselors of the political danger represented by Wyclif's teachings and requiring the English government to help suppress Wyclif.

What Wyclif represented for many sympathetic Englishmen, bouyant on the rising tide of antipapalism, was a theoretical basis for rejecting foreign authority claimed by the bishops of Rome. By Wyclif's "theory of dominion," the pontiff's power came not from God, but from the ancient Caesars of Rome. Therefore, what came from the papal chair must be wicked, for no wickedness could come from God. Such teachings directed against papal encroachment and "Caesarean" clergy gave Wyclif great popularity in London.

John of Gaunt had protected Wyclif, though his reasons for doing so were probably more political than religious. But King Richard II had a different notion. Once Wyclif's doctrines had been condemned by the

---

[9]See the text of Gregory's letter in Gee and Hardy, 105-108.

Convocation of Canterbury, Richard II issued letters patent against the followers of Wyclif, the so-called Lollards, at the insistence of Archbishop Courtenay. The letters authorized the arrest of Lollards until "they repent of the wickedness of their errors and heresies."[10]

Wyclif was nonetheless allowed to retire gracefully to his rectory at Lutterworth, in Leicestershire, where he spent the last months of his life writing tracts and other propaganda for his academic movement of "Poor Preachers" and promoting the so-called Wyclif Bible—the first full translation of the Bible from the Vulgate into English.[11] He died on the last day in the year 1384, still pastor at Lutterworth.

If by issuing his letters patent Richard II sought to placate Rome and relieve himself of pressure from that quarter, he was disillusioned. The Parliament, meeting at Cambridge in 1388, renewed complaints about provisions in the realm, and the pope reclaimed his right to make appointments to English bishoprics. Consequently, Parliament met at Westminster and renewed the Statute of Provisors (1351) with additional safeguards. This Second Statute of Provisors recited the first Provisors Act of Edward III and declared that it "holds always its force, and was never defeated, repealed, nor annulled in any point." Moreover, the king was "bound by his oath to cause the same to be kept as the law of his realm, though that by sufferance and negligence it has been since attempted to the contrary." Therefore, Parliament decreed

> that the free elections of archbishops, bishops, and all other dignities and benefices elective in England, shall hold from henceforth in the manner as they were granted by the king's progenitors, and the ancestors of other lords, founders.[12]

The Statute of Provisors further declared that should the pope make provision to an ecclesiastic in England, "in disturbance of the free elections," the king and his heirs assumed their right of presenting

---

[10]See the "Letters Patent Against the Lollards," in Gee and Hardy, 110-12.

[11]The New Testament is commonly accepted as Wyclif's own translation, the Old Testament, that of Nicholas of Hereford. The whole was revised around 1388. Even though the Wyclif Bible was suppressed in the fifteenth century, the survival of 150 manuscripts testifies to its tremendous popularity.

[12]See the "Second Statute of Provisors," in Gee and Hardy, 112-21.

benefices, "seeing that the election was first granted by the king's progenitors."

Rome replied by annulling not only the Second Statute of Provisors (1390), but also the first Provisors Act (1351) and the Statute of Carlisle (1307). It appeared that the pontiff would seek to penalize certain bishops for their part in carrying out the king's orders concerning royal nominees to the benefices. When the pope threatened to reduce the number of the king's counselors by translating bishops out of the realm, Parliament met the challenge in 1393 by passing the Second Statute of Praemunire forbidding cases claimed by royal jurisdiction from being appealed to Rome and forbidding the introduction of papal bulls and citations within the realm.[13]

A moderate compromise was reached in 1398 between Parliament and pope whereby the following items were agreed upon: When a bishopric falls vacant, the pope shall allow time for the election to be reported to Rome, whereupon he shall then provide the elect, if the king requests one, or he will appoint some other English subject acceptable to the king. The pope and the bishop shall take turns in appointing vacancies to cathedral and collegiate chapters until each shall have three turns, but no aliens except in the post of cardinals shall be appointed in England. Although Richard II was deposed during the next year,[14] the trouble about providing aliens became a dead issue from that time onward.

Another byproduct of the religious dispute between England and Rome was the emergence of Parliament as a powerful force to be reckoned with during the fourteenth century. As the king's power became more limited in the rise of Parliamentary government, the religious controversy could no longer be considered merely a dispute between king and pope over rival claims and jurisdictions. Parliament would also have to be considered. Parliament's protestation against papal encroachment on those customs, practices, and statutes of the realm which expressed the will and temperament of the English citizenry could no longer be ignored.

---

[13]See the full text of the "Second Statute of Praemunire," in Gee and Hardy, 122-25.

[14]The deposition is, of course, an important scene in Shakespeare's *Richard II* (1595-1596). King Richard's career also forms the basis for the play *Woodstock, or I Richard II* (c. 1592).

Upon the death of his father, John of Gaunt, Bolingbroke became the new Duke of Lancaster and returned from banishment to wrest his forfeited estates from the king's hands. But, finding popular support for his cause, Bolingbroke proceeded to lay claim to the crown on the grounds that Richard's tryanny had made Richard unworthy to administer affairs within the realm. Parliament met at the rebuilt Westminster Hall and there deposed Richard II as "altogether insufficient and unworthy." By the force of Parliament's decision, Bolingbroke ascended the English throne as King Henry IV (1399-1413).[15]

Less than three years after Henry IV came to the throne, Parliament took its first measure to suppress the Lollards by enacting the important statute *De Haeretico Comburendo*. It cited the "certain new sect" which, "against the law of God and of the Church," was then "usurping the office of preaching" by "dissembled holiness" and was teaching "divers new doctrines and wicked, heretical, and erroneous opinions" contrary to the determinations of the Holy Church. To spread their heresies, they "make unlawful conventicles and confederacies, they hold and exercise schools, they make and write books," and they "do daily perpetrate and commit other enormities horrible to be heard."[16]

Against these new heresies Parliament decreed that all such unauthorized activity cease. What is even more significant for later consideration is the penalty clause, which provided that those who refused to obey the statute were to be turned over to the secular court and "before the people, in a high place caused to be burnt, that such punishment may strike fear to the minds of others." It was, of course, a cruel and unjust act, and it was initiated by the king and his clergy against the followers of Wyclif. Far from silencing the Lollards, the act merely forced them underground from whence they would reappear with popular support during the English Reformation.

Meanwhile, after the statute *De Haeretico Comburendo* had been drawn up, but before it had become law, the Convocation brought proceedings against William Sawtre, a former chaplain who had relapsed

---

[15]His career forms the basis for Shakespeare's *Henry IV, Parts I and II* (1597-1598), but the force of Parliament seems pale compared to the Tudor political theory implied in the drama.

[16]See "*De Haeritico Comburendo*," in Gee and Hardy, 133-37.

into the Lollard heresy. After degrading him from clerical privilege, the Convocation procured a royal writ for his execution, and he became the first Lollard martyr.[17] But even such a harsh law could not extinguish the flame lit by Wyclif. By 1406 the Lollard teachings appeared unabated. In that year Prince Henry and the peers of the realm passed another statute against Lollards: offenders then became enemies of the state. In 1409, Archbishop Arundel issued new condemnations against Wyclif's doctrines and forbade the translation of the Bible without authority.

Like his father before him, Henry V was confronted with trouble from the Lollards. Sir John Oldcastle, Baron Cobham (1377-1417), a leader of the Lollards, found himself out of grace with the young king. Oldcastle, as "leader and captain" of his Lollard followers, used his Kentish castle of Cowling as headquarters. In 1413, the Convocation cited him as the principal protector of the heretical sect, which denied to the bishops their right to forbid unauthorized preaching.

The bishops, spurred on by Arundel, convened and called upon King Henry to arrest Oldcastle. When Henry delayed taking positive action, Arundel summoned Oldcastle before an ecclesiastical court and convicted him of heresy. With these sustained pressures from the clergy, Henry ordered Oldcastle to the Tower with the promise of release upon recantation.

But the Lollard leader broke out of the Tower and organized an armed rebellion. When Henry learned of the coup, he ordered royal troops to attack an assembly of Lollards at St. Giles's fields. Those who were not slain on the spot were taken prisoner. Thirty were hanged for treason, seven were burned alive for heresy, and thirty-two were fined and imprisoned. Oldcastle again escaped and spent the next three years consorting with the king's enemies in a conspiracy to overthrow the government.

Meanwhile, Parliament passed another heresy act in 1414 which empowered royal officers to arrest heretics and hand them over to the bishops for trial in the ecclesiastical courts. When Oldcastle was again

---

[17]Sawtre offended the Holy Church by declaring that he would not worship "the cross on which Christ suffered, but only Christ himself who had suffered on the cross." Worse yet, he denied the doctrine of transubstantiation. He was burned alive at Smithfield to the great delight of a multitude of spectators. See the "Royal Writ for the Burning of Sawtre" (26 February 1401), in Gee and Hardy, 138-39.

captured—this time in Wales—and taken to London, he himself became a martyr for Lollard beliefs.[18]

Henry V's death in 1422 brought his eight-month-old son to the throne. By terms of the royal will, the government would be administered by the late king's brothers: John of Bedford as governor of Normandy and Regent of France, and Humphrey of Gloucester as Regent of England during the long minority of Henry VI (1422-1461).[19] Parliament, however, set aside the late Henry's will, perhaps led by Henry's uncle, Henry Beaufort, bishop of Winchester, and they made Bedford the real protector of the realm, while the powers of government were entrusted to a Parliamentary council.

Beaufort recognized in Gloucester a possible threat to the young king and took measures to reduce that danger. As Chancellor of the realm, Beaufort became the real power behind the Parliamentary Council, but Gloucester returned to England in an effort to undermine his uncle Henry Beaufort and pursue his own ambitious plans. Gloucester spurred the men of London to attack Beaufort's palace in Southwark in 1425; that not enough, he made an unsuccessful charge against Bishop Beaufort before the Parliament.

In France, Beaufort had accepted the dignity of cardinal and papal legate. It was unfortunate in that Beaufort now withdrew from the Council and allowed Gloucester to pursue his unscrupulous plans. Duke Humphrey made good use of the opportunity by appealing to the anti-papal party within the realm in an effort to discredit Beaufort. His success in this endeavor can be measured by the document known as "Remonstrance Against Legatine Powers of Cardinal Beaufort" (1428).[20] In this document, "Prince Hymphry" declared that according to ancient custom "no legate of the Apostolic See ought to come into the kingdom

---

[18]Sir John Oldcastle, Baron Cobham, originally inspired Falstaff in Shakespeare's *Henry IV, Parts I and II*. He also appears in *The Famous Victories of Henry V* (c. 1588). Oldcastle's character is vindicated in the Admiral's Men's play *Sir John Oldcastle* (1599) by Munday, Drayton, Wilson, and Hathaway.

[19]The events of his reign form the basis for Shakespeare's *Henry VI, Parts I, II, and III* (1591-1592).

[20]See the "Remonstrance Against the Legatine Powers of Cardinal Beaufort," in Gee and Hardy, 139-41.

of England . . . save at the bidding, asking, request, invitation, or entreaty of the king of England."

Cardinal Beaufort, according to the document, had entered the
realm without the king's permission and, therefore, was forbidden to exercise his legatine powers. Gloucester apparently hoped to renew his
claims to the Council by this remonstrance more than he hoped to ini-
tiate further ecclesiastical controversy with Rome. Nevertheless, Beaufort became the victor and succeeded in regaining control of the royal
council.[21]

By this time the state of the Church in England was largely decadent.
Clergymen had forfeited moral leadership among the people as Lollards
and anticlerical factions drew attention to their loose living and low
moral standards. Superstition and sorcery became increasingly a part of
the national scene. For example, Eleanor Cobham, wife of Duke Humphrey, was accused of attempting to destroy young Henry's life by melt-
ing a wax image of the king over a fire in 1441. For her "sorcery" she was
required to do penance by walking barefoot through the city for three
days, wrapped in a sheet and carrying a candle; thereafter, she was imprisoned for life.[22] Jeanne D'Arc had been burned at Rouen a decade
earlier on the charge of sorcery. The magical incantations of Friar Bungay were already legendary.[23] The Church in England was suffering from
the general confusion of the times, both spiritually and intellectually,
and the times were ripe for reformation.

Dissipated and worn down by self-indulgence, King Edward IV
died in the spring of 1483, barely forty years old.[24] His twelve-year-old

---

[21]Cardinal Beaufort plays a significant part in Shakespeare's *Henry VI, Parts I and
II*. He also appears in *The Blind Beggar of Bednal Green* (c. 1600) by John Day and
Henry Chettle, but this play is a historical romance rather than a chronicle play. Both
plays make him more villainous than the historical documents warrant. The latter play
particularly derogates his character by making him a rival for the affections of Lady
Eleanor.

[22]The story of Eleanor Cobham appears in Shakespeare's *Henry VI, Part II*.

[23]His reputation is confirmed in Robert Greene's play, *Friar Bacon and Friar Bungay*
(1594).

[24]The two parts of Thomas Heywood's *Edward IV* (1599) are based upon the life of
Edward. There is also an account of Mistress Jane Shore, which is reminiscent of
Eleanor Cobham's lamentable condition. In the second part, Doctor Shaw, the king's
confessor, is a familiar priest of the Old Faith whose rascality is exploited for effect.

son succeeded him on the throne as Edward V (9 April-25 June 1483). Richard, Duke of Gloucester, the young king's uncle, was named Protector of the Realm by act of the Council, and young Edward was lodged in the Tower.

Richard's personal ambitions to wear the crown himself, however, soon became apparent, and he set himself against the Queen Mother's party by an accusation of sorcery, thrusting forth his withered arm as evidence. Further, he declared that the late king's marriage was illegal; therefore, young Edward was not entitled to wear the crown. The result was that on 25 June 1483 representatives of the realm assembled and asked Richard to be king. He graciously consented and was crowned within two weeks as Richard III (1483-1485).

Richard's pretensions of reform were quickly unmasked; at the beginning of 1485 he broke his own statutes by levying "benevolences" for his treasury. To appease the Yorkists he determined to marry his own niece, Elizabeth. This series of moves, along with the growing report of Richard's alleged villainy in murdering the two royal princes, greatly reduced the number of his followers.[25]

When Henry Tudor, Earl of Richmond, crossed the Channel and landed a force at Milford Haven in August 1485, he found a ready following among those who wished to be free of an "unnatural tryant." Henry Tudor is said to have recited from the Forty-third Psalm, "Judge me, O God, plead my cause against an ungodly nation," as he knelt down to kiss the soil, determined to deliver England in the name of God and St. George.

Marching his men eastward, Henry engaged Richard near Leicester and defeated him at Bosworth Field on 22 August 1485. Sir William Stanley lifted Richard's crown from beneath a hawthorn bush and placed it on the head of the victor while the soldiers on the field acknowledged him as King Henry VII. This event, although only indirectly related at this point, had tremendous importance for the religious controversy during the next century. From the time of Henry's victory at Bosworth Field, Tudor dramatists had a constant bias in their plays.

---

[25]The anonymous play *The True Tragedy of Richard III* (1589) is based on his career, as is Shakespeare's *Richard III* (1592-1593). He also appears in Shakespeare's *Henry VI, Parts II and III*.

CHAPTER II

EARLY TUDOR
CONTROVERSIES
WITH ROME

Throughout the fifteenth century the Church had become largely dependent upon the Crown for protection against Lollards and antipapal magnates. In doing so, the Church lost much of the power and influence it once exercised in England. Even popes of the Reniassance had not been able to command much respect from the faithful because of Church excesses and unholy examples.

The corruption and abuses of succeeding popes are a matter of record. Innocent VIII (1484-1492) achieved infamy by trying to advance his children with worldly possessions and by padding his treasury through proceeds from the sale of offices. For family reasons, Innocent made Giovanni de Medici (afterwards Leo X) a cardinal at the age of thirteen. Pope Alexander VI (1492-1503), after gaining his chair through bribery, achieved notoriety by arranging propitious marriages for his illegitimate daughter, Lucrezia Borgia. For his illegitimate son, Cesare Borgia, he created a principality out of the states of the Church.[1] Julius II (1503-

---

[1]Barnaby Barnes's play *Devil's Charter* (1607) is based on the popular legend that Pope Alexander VI sold his soul to the devil in exchange for the triple crown. A dumb show depicts Lucifer offering him the mitre. Cesare, the pope's son, kills his own brother; Lucretia, the pope's daughter, murders her husband. Cesare also provides a catalogue of his father's crimes.

1513) sincerely tried to advance the temporal powers of the papacy by personally leading his soldiers onto the field of battle dressed in full armor. With men such as these as the earthly heads of the Church, it is little wonder that the office of Vicar of Christ had suffered and was unable to inspire absolute moral confidence among English citizens at large.

The moral chaos of the times was reflected in the English Church. Among secular clergy, benefices were bought and sold without apology, ignorance prevailed, and money was extorted from the laity through the abuse of the confessional and Church discipline. Religious houses became characterized by luxury and unparalleled extravagance. Friars, especially, were cited for their notorious corruption, indolence, and self-indulgence. Chantry priests, generally at their leisure for dissipation, represented a large part of the clergy. Pilgrimages to sacred shrines had become compulsory despite the unreasonable claims such places made for their relics as a means of attracting pilgrims and extracting money to fill their coffers. Even Archbishop Arundel declared, "Holy Church hath determined that it is needful for a Christian man to go a pilgrimage to holy places, and there especially to worship holy relics of saints, apostles, martyrs, confessors, and all saints approved by the Church of Rome."[2]

Loyal sons of the Holy Church, such as Erasmus, would find the veneration of relics untenable. John Heywood and John Bale among contemporary playwrights would parody the claims of holy relics for comic effect. The time seemed right for religious reformation if the Church in England was to exercise appreciable influence over the lives of Englishmen at large and perceptive scholars at Oxford at the dawn of the English Renaissance.

Henry VII, since he claimed succession to the throne through his mother's line going back to John of Gaunt, quickly sought to make his somewhat tenuous position as king secure. Calling Parliament into session in 1485, he gained from that body his right to wear the crown for himself and his heirs. By his marriage to Elizabeth, eldest daughter of Edward IV, he strengthened his position through popular support dur-

---

[2]William Clark, *The Anglican Reformation* (New York: Charles Scribner's Sons, 1901) 54.

ing the following year. This accomplished, he made his reign absolutely secure by extracting from the pope a bull recognizing his title in 1486. If others of his followers were not satisfied by these measures, he probably removed the last obstacle to their absolute obedience in 1495 by leading Parliament to enact legislation making it clear that to obey a *de facto* king was not treason.

Although the first Tudor king did not himself enter into controversy with Rome, he initiated, for political reasons, two marriages which would play strategic parts in future religious disputes. Envisioning an end to future trouble with the Scots, he married his daughter Margaret to King James IV of Scotland in 1502, but it is unlikely that he ever anticipated a Scottish king and heir upon the throne of England in little more than a century. A few months earlier, Henry married his son and heir apparent Arthur to Catherine, daughter of Ferdinand of Aragon and Isabella of Castile. His political intentions there were quashed, however, when Arthur died within less than six months after the wedding.

Failing in his effort to marry Catherine himself, and unsuccessful even in marrying Catherine's half-witted sister Joanna, Henry succeeded in gaining papal dispensation allowing his second son, the future Henry VIII, to marry Arthur's widow. The marriage took place two months after Henry VIII's accession.

If Henry VII became increasingly despotic and grasping in his last years on the throne, he at least attempted to ward off trouble from Rome by appointing clergymen for his counselors, going on religious pilgrimages, establishing religious foundations, and enacting a law against usury whereby offenders would be punished by Church courts. Yet, despite these measures toward ecclesiastical conformity, the Oxford Reformers were already at work spreading the New Learning in England which would soon provide an intellectual basis for the complete separation of the Church in England and the Roman Curia.

When Henry VII died in 1509, he was succeeded by his eighteen-year-old son, Henry VIII (1509-1547). Skilled in the art of self-defense, athletic, and handsomest of the princes in Europe, Henry VIII was no less accomplished in the New Learning. Indeed, the Oxford Reformers recognized in the new king a kindred spirit able to promote reform throughout the realm.

By 1512 that reformation may be said to have begun in earnest when John Colet addressed the Convocation of the Clergy setting forth the religious ideal of the Oxford Reformers in his "Great Sermon on the Extirpation of Heresy."

> Would that for once you would remember your name and profession and take thought for the reformation of the Church! Never was it more necessary, and never did the state of the church need more vigorous endeavours. . . . We are troubled with heretics, but no heresy of theirs is so fatal to us and to the people at large as the vicious and depraved lives of the clergy. That is the worst heresy of all.[3]

For his bold utterance, Colet was charged with heresy by the bishop of London, although both Archbishop William Warham and King Henry protected and defended him. The young king even went so far as to call Colet his own "doctor."

Yet, Henry VIII was early a paragon of orthodoxy and a supporter of the papacy. While the Oxford Reformers were developing a critical spirit of examination aimed at reducing current abuses and advocating a return to the pristine purity of the Church, Henry seemed to favor the status quo. He was openly pious, attended Mass daily—even on days he hunted—and listened intently to sermons. The pope rewarded him in 1510 with the Golden Rose, and in 1513 with the word and cap of maintenance. In 1521, Henry published *The Defense of the Seven Sacraments* in answer to Luther's heresies, for which Pope Leo X recognized the English kings's loyalty to the Holy Church by bestowing the title *Defensor Fidei*.[4] Subsequent monarchs of England have continued to bear that title.

Oxford Reformers and patrons of the New Learning in England set themselves to the task of purifying the Church and returning it to the spiritual ideals of earlier times rather than perpetuating commentaries of Church Fathers and theological disputes of scholastics. Particular abuses were called into question, such as the sale of indulgences, a problem which even Chaucer had exposed in the fourteenth century, as well as clerical immorality, worldliness, and indolence.

----

[3]John Richard Green, *History of the English People* (New York: Harper & Bros., 1900-1903) 2:87-88.

[4]Wolsey and Gardiner discuss King Henry's acquisition of this title in *When You See Me You Know Me* (1604-1605) by William Rowley.

Erasmus had earlier joined the temper of the movement by drawing attention to a general depravity of the Church with the publication of his devotional manual *Enchiridion Militis Christiani* (1501) even before Henry VIII ascended the throne. Erasmus attacked superstition, adoration of relics, pilgrimages, and lip service to God. Such open criticism, together with the famous edition of the New Testament in original Greek, the *Novum Instrumentum* (1516), represented the proverbial egg which Erasmus laid but which Luther hatched.

It may be that expediency led King Henry VIII from his apparent orthodoxy into the religious dispute with Rome. Certainly the notorious divorce from Catherine of Aragon provided a *cause celèbre* for his growing absolutist policy in the administration of the realm. Henry's marriage to his deceased brother's widow—she was six years his senior—resulted in the birth of several children between the years 1510 and 1518, although only Princess Mary survived.

When it became apparent that Henry would probably not produce a male heir by Catherine, the English king broke from her. If a papal dispensation could make the originally noncanonical marriage legal, Henry reasoned, a papal dispensation could surely rectify what he saw as a threat to the Tudor dynasty—the absence of a male heir. Appealing to orthodoxy, Henry announced that his failure to produce a male heir must be God's judgment upon his noncanonical marriage, and he instituted divorce proceedings in 1527.

Thomas Wolsey (1475?-1530), archbishop of York, cardinal, Lord Chancellor, and papal legate, obediently summoned Henry before his legatine court on the charge of living in adultery with his late brother's wife. The technicalities of the case would have no doubt insured Henry's success, except for one obstacle—Catherine's obstinacy. Wolsey suggested that the case be referred out of the realm for settlement in Rome. But Wolsey's solution to the problem was to marry Henry to Renée, daughter of King Louis XII—a solution contrary to Henry's design. Henry, therefore, bypassed Wolsey and sent his own commission to procure from the pope a nullification of the marriage and a dispensation to marry Anne Boleyn.

Pope Clement VII (1523-1534) was faced with more than a mere matter of canonical law: Catherine of Aragon was the aunt of Emperor Charles V, and Charles had that very year sacked Rome and besieged the papal palace. Clement suggested that the case be settled by papal legates in England, if they could not first dissuade Henry from his purpose. Simultaneously, Clement assured the emperor that Catherine would not suffer and that the case would be tried in Rome.

A series of vain disputes took place before legate Campeggio was forced to consent to a trial of the divorce case. The trial opened at Blackfriar's on the last day of May in the year 1529. King Henry and his wife were summoned by the middle of June. When it became clear that the dispute would not be settled easily, Clement VII called the case before the papal court in Rome. Henry realized that his only hope for success then rested in forcing a settlement in his own law courts.

To the delight of English clergy and laity alike, Henry cited Wolsey under the Statute of Praemunire in October 1529 for breaking the laws of the realm by exercising legatine powers. Thus humiliated and broken in spirit, Wolsey died the following year en route to the Tower under a charge of treasonable correspondence with the French ambassador. His dying words have become immortal: "If I had served my God as diligently as I have done the King, He would not have given me over in my gray hairs."[5]

Meanwhile, with Wolsey out of the way, two other men rose to prominence under Henry's administration, and they both proposed solutions of their own for the king's divorce. Thomas Cranmer (1489-1556), later to become archbishop of Canterbury, suggested that the question of the validity of the marriage be settled by scholars of the universities. Should they decide against the suit, the matter could be submitted to the law courts of the realm. Thomas Cromwell (1485?-1540), later to become vice-regent of ecclesiastical affairs, suggested that Henry throw off the authority of the pope and declare himself supreme head (administrator) of the Church of England. He further argued that the state was obliged to perform the will of its prince. Apparently Cromwell's solution suited Henry's design, and he summoned Parliament in November 1529 to settle matters.

At the same time, Pope Clement alienated many English citizens when he aligned himself with Emperor Charles V. The pope had failed to understand the strong national sentiment among Englishmen, a force

---

[5]Wolsey's unpopular administration may have suggested Skelton's *Magnificence* (1516). Wolsey's fall is dramatized in Shakespeare's *Henry VIII*.

which had resisted temporal claims from stronger pontiffs than Clement. The trouble at this point cannot be considered a purely religious issue, free from politics—neither on the part of Henry nor Clement. Had Henry not moved on the tide of rising nationalism, his dispute with Rome would have been doomed from the start.

The so-called Reformation Parliament (1529-1536) dealt with problems of clerical abuses. It sought to limit the rights of the clergy and to free laymen from clerical oppression. The new chancellor, Sir Thomas More (1478-1535), himself a layman, ironically delivered the opening speech, 3 November 1529, declaring that of all matters of state, those concerning clerics most needed reform. During the next seven years, ecclesiastical reform occupied parliamentary legislation to an unprecedented extent. Bills were enacted regulating the practice of mortuaries, probate fees charged by bishops, pluralities, and nonresidence.

If Henry's Reformation Parliament was to succeed in its initial objective, some power greater than Commons would be necessary before the clergy could admit the need for any reformation. That stronger power proved to be the king himself. Unsatisfied with the bishops' failure to recognize the source of much contention among the English laity, Henry demanded that the clergy recognize the king of England as the Supreme Head of the Church of England. By calling the clergy into submission to the king's governance of the Church in England, not only could reformation proceed unimpeded by episcopal opposition, but the bishops and primates would be forced to look directly to the king for approval rather than to the papacy. The implications were clear enough to Lord Chancellor Thomas More, for on the day following the submission of the clergy he resigned the chancellorship.[6]

Archbishop Warham's death in 1532 had brought to the primacy the man of Henry's own choosing, Thomas Cranmer, a theologian in the humanistic tradition of Erasmus. Cranmer, since about 1525, had prayed for the overthrow of papal authority over the Church, and his reverence for the New Learning and the study of scriptures had lent reinforcement

---

[6]Thomas More's life inspired the drama *The Book of Sir Thomas More* (c. 1600-1601), probably by Anthony Munday, Henry Chettle, Thomas Heywood, and William Shakespeare.

to his point of view.[7] Yet, Pope Clement VII provided Cranmer with the see, and he was consecrated in January 1533 by the bishop of London.

By previous arrangement with the king, Archbishop Cranmer wrote Henry a letter twelve days after his consecration asking for permission to examine the matter of the king's divorce and passing final judgment on it. Permission was granted, and the case opened on 10 May 1533. Catherine refused the summons to appear. Thirteen days later the archbishop pronounced Henry's marriage to Catherine null and void. Within another five days, Cranmer declared Henry's marriage to Anne Boleyn legal and binding.

Of utmost importance for the religious dispute at its most crucial point was the Restraint of Appeals which Parliament enacted in 1533. That statute is probably no more than the logical extension of the Statute of Praemunire, but it became the legal principle behind Henry's reformation of the Church in England. It was, in fact, a reaffirmation of ancient royal prerogatives in England before the bishop of Rome assumed those prerogatives. It also embodied the important principle of the divine right of kings, who rule in their realms by God's grace and not by permission of Rome. It further prohibited appeals to Rome in all cases determinable by royal law courts, both temporal and spiritual. By appealing to ancient prerogatives of kings in England and various parliamentary acts, the Restraint of Appeals can be seen from the Anglican point of view as a perfectly legal, logical, and traditional document rather than as a revolutionary rejection of papal authority.[8]

Meanwhile, Clement VII retaliated against Archbishop Cranmer's judgment of the divorce case by excommunicating Cranmer, together with all bishops who had taken part in the trial. Another bull issued on the same day, 4 July 1533, excommunicated King Henry, unless he would agree to leave Anne and return to Catherine, his only legal wife.

Henry answered Clement by calling for a General Council and withdrawing the English ambassadors from Rome. The die was cast. Perhaps Clement had merely been goaded into doing precisely what Henry hoped

---

[7]Cranmer is the hero in Shakespeare's *Henry VIII*.

[8]For a detailed examination of the discussions behind and leading up to this statute, see G. R. Elton, "The Evolution of a Reformation Statute," *EHR* 64 (April 1949): 174-79.

he would do—force Henry's subjects to choose between their sovereign king and a foreign potentate. Accordingly, Henry set into operation a well-calculated program of antipapal propaganda. Henry gave instructions to the clergy that sermons should be preached throughout the realm showing that the pope was subject to the General Council in the administration of the English national Church and that Clement could not lawfully claim any more jurisdiction in England than could any other foreign bishops. The Statute of Appeals was posted on every church door. Foreseeing a possible show of force from papal allies, Henry sent envoys to Germany ready to propose an alliance with the Protestant princes.

The last of a series of ecclesiastical bills enacted by Parliament in the spring of 1534 was the important First Act of Succession, so called because it was the first act in English history that regulated the succession to the throne. Since previous legislation had removed papal control over ecclesiastical administration of the Church of England, the Act of Succession seemed to make the breach with Rome complete. In this case the pope was expressly forbidden to interfere with the natural order of succession to the English throne as former popes had presumed to do. By terms of the Act of Succession, should Henry and Anne Boleyn fail to produce a male heir, the succession fell to Princess Elizabeth, the only legitimate heir. Thereafter, the public at large was required to take an oath to observe the Act of Succession upon pain of forfeiture or life imprisonment, and those guilty of slandering the king's marriage to Anne Boleyn automatically became guilty of high treason.

Before Henry's breach with Rome it had been an act of heresy to supplant the pope with any other authority. But a new bill was enacted which not only recognized Henry as Supreme Head of the Church of England, but also gave license to all future verbal abuse of the pope: "No manner of speaking . . . against the said Bishop of Rome or his pretended power . . . nor . . . against any laws called spiritual laws made by his authority and repugnant to the English laws or the King's prerogative shall be deemed . . . heresy." This saving act was particularly useful to dramatists during the polemical period when the stage plays were especially vitriolic in their abuse of the pope.

The Convocation of Canterbury met in 1534 to consider the repudiation of all papal jurisdiction in the Church of England. The question presented to the clergy was whether or not God had bestowed on the Roman pontiff any greater jurisdiction over the realm of England than any other foreign bishop. A vote was taken, and the Convocation answered in the negative by a vote of thirty-four to four in the Lower House. The Convocation of York considered the same question and agreed with Canterbury unanimously.

Thus far, Henry's design was as nearly perfect in its execution as possible. All of Parliament and the Convocations of both Canterbury and York had recognized no power within the realm greater than the king. Incidentally, it should be noted that the important Protestant principle of scriptural authority was stated explicitly. John Bale, for one, would make effective use of this point in his polemical drama, as would Nathaniel Wood.

Meanwhile, pressed by Henry's flagrant disregard of papal claims in the matter of the divorce case, the cardinals at Rome met in consistory on 23 March 1534 and there issued a unanimous verdict against the king's divorce. They decreed that Henry was to reinstate Catherine and compensate her for financial losses and court fees during the trial.

When the news of the cardinals' decision reached London, Henry responded by directing all English preachers to preach sermons decrying the pope's usurpation of royal prerogatives. Considering the fact that sermons were then the most effective means of disseminating official information, it was a vital move on Henry's part. What Rome would continue to consider a matter of religious heresy, the reformed clergy and English subjects would consider a threat to national independence— Henry would see to that.

During the summer of 1534, English subjects, both spiritual and temporal, were required to subscribe to the new oath of allegiance recognizing Henry as Supreme Head of the Church of England and acknowledging the new ecclesiastical policies enacted by Parliament. This was done rather easily, although Sir Thomas More and the bishop of Rochester refused to sign, for which they were sent to the Tower.

When Parliament finished its legislation in November 1534, Henry's monumental claims over the ecclesiastical policies and administration of the Church of England were complete. Papal authority within the realm had been virtually abolished, the clergy had recognized no power under Christ greater than the king, and the threat of high treason secured allegiance from English citizens at large.

A Tudor reign of terror against recusants stained the early months of 1535 with unprecedented atrocities aimed at English subjects who balked at Henry's reformation of the Church. Thomas Cromwell, as vicar-general, goaded Henry into punishing all offenders to the fullest extent permitted by recent legislation. When the question of the king's supremacy over the Church was asked of Thomas More at his trial, he remained silent and refused to reply. Once judged guilty, More broke his silence by attacking the Act of Supremacy as repugnant to the Holy Church and the laws of God. At his death he announced from the scaffold that he would die in and for the faith of the Holy Catholic Church, apart from which there could be no salvation.

Pope Paul III (1534-1549) had, on 30 August 1535, issued his bull *Eius qui immobilis*, which excommunicated Henry, declared him deposed, and laid England under interdict. All the king's men were thus released from oaths of fidelity, and they were ordered not to obey his commands any longer. But Henry was not King John, and no prince in Europe was prepared to execute the papal bull.

When a series of armed uprisings broke out in the north, Henry found reasonable justification for extending his law dissolving the lesser monasteries (1536) to those larger houses formerly untouched by parliamentary legislation. New legislation would be forthcoming, since laws suppressing monasteries and other religious houses were passed in 1539. With the final surrender of Waltham in the spring of 1540, the last of the English abbeys felt the full weight of royal supremacy. The dissolution of the monasteries dispossessed some 8,000 monks, canons, and friars.

Another significant phase of Henry's reformation was directed against various shrines. Certain venerable sites were exposed as frauds, such as the "Rood of Grace" at Boxley in Kent. What had formerly been an inexplicable phenomenon, in which the corpus moved its eyes and lips on the cross, was then exposed as a work of deception in which the "miraculous" was effected by concealed wires.

Perhaps the most celebrated attack on religious shrines was the one that spoiled the tomb of Thomas Becket at Canterbury. Not only were that martyr's bones burned publicly, but loads of jewels, gold, and silver were taken from the shrine upon its dissolution in 1538. Even Becket's name was erased from the service books because he was considered a traitor by standards of the new faith. All such shrines were regarded as tending toward idolatry and superstition and, therefore, had to be destroyed in the name of purity. All relics were ordered thrown down and shrines leveled.

The Bible came to be part of the general Reformation program. By appealing directly to it rather than to Church tradition, Reformers were able to circumvent much of what they considered to be "Romish" interpolations. Cromwell ordered the Bible to be placed in every church for public perusal. If the Reformation was to be a return to apostolic Christianity, there could be no more authoritative source for a Church free from Roman innovation than what was described in the simple words of the original documents in their English translation.

No one, not even the king himself, could have anticipated the excesses to which the practice of lay Bible reading for sole authority in ecclesiastical practices would soon lead the nation. Controversy quickly arose over the individual interpretation of certain texts. Even the Mass, the most important part of the Catholic service, was attacked as little more, according to scriptural precedent, than a Romanist innovation. Transubstantiation, still part of canonical law under Henry's administration, was profanely ridiculed in ballads and plays. The sacred words of the consecration, "*Hoc est corpus,*" were reduced by ridicule and parody to "hocus-pocus."

Yet Henry was never quite prepared to effect the full, logical consequence of his reformation. After all, his argument was with papal authority within the realm and not with Church dogma. The Church of England, as he saw it, was still the Holy Catholic Church in faith and practice, but it could no longer be in any sense Roman Catholic. Just how seriously Henry regarded this conception of the Church of England is nowhere more evident than in the Six Articles Act which he personally pushed through Parliament in 1539.

The Six Articles Act, known popularly among extreme Protestants as the "Bloody Act" or the "Whip with Six Stings," was too reactionary for some enthusiasts of the Reformation because it seemed practically the same in form as what the pope upheld, except in that papal claims to authority were omitted in the act. Foxes's *Book of Martyrs*, from the bishop of London's register, gives the details of a general enforcement of the act in 1541, with the names of 208 indicted for treason. Among those indicted was a keeper of the Carpenter's Hall cited for permitting an Interlude "wherein priests are railed on."

With the fall and execution of Cromwell in 1540,[9] Henry was more than ever Supreme Head of the Church of England. Each ecclesiastic within the realm derived from the king his right to serve. It was the Supreme Head alone who seemed able to define orthodoxy and heresy.

But Henry's last years failed to bring about either reconciliation with Roman Catholic Europe or the ecclesiastical harmony at home he had desired. Even the *King's Book* (1543), which set forth "a true and perfect doctrine for all his people," was not enough to quash the rising dissent. With his national Church in a state of unrest, Henry VIII died on 28 January 1547, firmly supported by the great majority of his subjects. The triumph of Protestantism would follow, though only for a brief interval.

Henry's son by Jane Seymour came to the throne on 20 February 1547 as Edward VI.[10] Almost at once a host of varied theological beliefs poured into England, adding to the general confusion in ecclesiastical disputes. Lutherans, Calvinists, and Zwinglians, in particular, contributed to the theological dissension, although only the Calvinists seemed to have influenced the nation to any great degree.

In an effort to check the several extremes that were apparent in ecclesiastical affairs, the Council began to look for some stabilizing measures. One came in July 1547 when Cranmer issued the *Book of Homilies*. Originally designed as a book of sermons to be preached by clerics who lacked the ability to compose their own, the *Book of Homilies* soon became an official program of the Reformation when the king's government ordered that they be preached each Sunday. Cranmer's preface described the "manifold enormities" which had entered the Church through "the false usurped power of the bishop of Rome," turning men from true religion "unto popish superstition." The homilies, therefore, were an effort to correct "enormities" and to provide men with an understanding of primitive Christianity.

---

[9]The story of Cromwell is dramatized in *Thomas Lord Cromwell* (c. 1600). It was based on Foxe's account in the *Book of Martyrs*. According to the play, Bishop Gardiner bribes two disreputable fellows to bear false witness against Cromwell, a hero of the English Reformation. After the two false informers have accused Cromwell, Bishop Gardiner lifts his crucifix and grants them absolution from their sin of perjury.

[10]By an act of Parliament in 1544, the line of succession was settled so that the crown would pass to Edward upon Henry's death. Should Edward die without issue, Mary would inherit the throne; should Mary prove childless, Elizabeth, the daughter of Anne Boleyn, would succeed as next in line.

One month after the *Book of Homilies* was issued, a general visitation
was ordered throughout the realm, and ecclesiastical visitors were provided with Royal Injunctions forbidding all pilgrimages and command-
ing the destruction of all shrines, stained glass windows, paintings
representing objects of religious veneration, carvings, and images. English was to be used in the service, the Great Bible was to be provided
for lay reading, a copy of Erasmus's *Paraphrases* upon the Gospels (in
English) was to be read in the services, and royal supremacy was to be
acknowledged. Royal Injunctions did away with certain Roman customs, such as "creeping to the cross" on Good Friday and the use of
ashes, palms, candles, and holy water. Instead of the procession before
the Sunday High Mass, the new litany was to sing or say, "From the tyranny of the Bishop of Rome and all his detestable enormities, Good
Lord, deliver us."

Cranmer and other bishops and learned men soon entered upon a
project to create a new order of public worship in the English language.
The result of their collaboration was the *First Prayer Book of King Edward VI*. More than any single act of legislation, this work articulated
the Reformation of the Church of England. It represented the English
mind at work in selecting the forms suitable for the English religious
temperament, and it was phrased in noble, elevating, and powerful
prose. But the doctrinal changes reflected in it go far beyond Henry's
boldest design in separating the Church of England from Roman
control.

CHAPTER III

ELIZABETHAN
SETTLEMENT OF RELIGION

The Protestant Reformation of the Church of England was cut short by the death of Edward VI in 1553, and Mary Tudor ascended the throne. During her stormy five-year reign, the nation surrendered the Church of England to Rome and again recognized papal supremacy. This reversal seems to have been Mary's ruling passion.

Queen Mary's First Proclamation About Religion (1553) called attention to the common use of drama for propaganda and ordered such practices to cease. Sedition and false rumors circulating in publications and stage plays were prohibited, as were printing and all stage interludes, without special permission from the queen.

The nation as a whole may have been relatively indifferent concerning which form of worship was to be observed in the churches on Sundays and holy days, but it could not remain indifferent to the violence that characterized the next four years of attempts to restore Roman Catholicism to England. The lamentable events that followed the revival of heresy laws earned the queen the infamous label "Bloody Mary," which lingers in popular references to the zealously pious sovereign to this day.

The Marian Persecution may stand out in English history for its cruelty and inhumanity in the name of religion because of the indelible impression left upon the consciousness of Anglicans by John Foxe's *Book of Martyrs*.[1] His martyrology became required reading for congregations in the late sixteenth and early seventeenth centuries. As anti-Romanist propaganda it became an effective and monumental account of those years when human beings were burned alive at Smithfield by Mary Tudor's order.[2]

Queen Mary's zeal in restoring England to papal control created an understandable bifurcation among her subjects. It was in the midst of rising dissent, aware of the failure of her governmental and ecclesiastical policies, that Mary Tudor died on 17 November 1558. According to her own request, she was not buried in the stately robes befitting a queen, but in the simple habit of a nun. She had been a devout woman with a sincere mission, but her unpopular marriage to Philip II of Spain and her zeal to extirpate heresy had estranged her from the affections of her subjects. She would always be "Bloody Mary" to the English.[3]

Elizabeth I (1558-1603) was proclaimed queen amid the general rejoicing of those who had found Mary Tudor's excesses unbearable.[4] But

---

[1]John Foxe, in the company of Alexander Nowell and John Bale, became a Protestant convert while at Oxford. Leaving England in the first year of Mary's reign, he associated with radical Protestants on the Continent. At Basel he published the original version of his martyrology in Latin in 1559. After his ordination in England he produced a more elaborate English version in 1563.

[2]The first of the Protestants burned was John Rogers, a former priest responsible for the edition of the Bible ordered by Henry VIII to be placed in all churches. He was burned alive on 4 February 1555, in the presence of his eleven children, because he refused to repudiate the past twenty years and return to the true faith.

[3]The first part of Thomas Heywood's *If You Know Not Me You Know Nobody* (1603-1605) deals with the Marian Persecution when a Kentishman is punished for offering a petition to the queen on behalf of his countrymen for whom religious liberty had been promised in view of their service to the Crown. In Thomas Dekker's *Whore of Babylon* (1607), a dumb show depicts a clerical procession leading the corpse of Queen Mary with a group of blindfolded counselors following behind; but Truth wakes up and removes their blindfolds.

[4]Heywood's *If You Know Not Me* also deals with the early life of Elizabeth. Through a dumb show, it portrays an attempt to assassinate the queen by several monks led by Bishop Gardiner; but they are driven back by guardian angels. In another scene the Lord Mayor of London presents her with a Bible on her triumphal entry.

the new queen faced a nation torn asunder by religious strife. A firm policy on the settlement of religion was necessary, but those in charge of ecclesiastical administration within the realm were probably ready to resist any change of the status quo. To add to the general religious confusion, Reformers exiled during the period of Mary's persecution began to return to England, bringing with them Protestant doctrines and theories of ecclesiastical polity from the Continent.

The queen's first Parliament met in January 1559 and sat until the end of April when the Elizabethan Settlement of Religion was finally effected. The bill that required the greatest amount of attention was the Act of Supremacy. Originally called "The Bill for the Supremacy of the Churches of England and Ireland, and Abolishing of the Pope of Rome," the Act of Supremacy repealed the Heresy Act of Philip and Mary and abolished papal jurisdiction in the realm. In addition, all ecclesiastics and temporal officials were required to take the Oath of Supremacy recognizing the queen as supreme "governor" in all temporal, spiritual, and ecclesiastical matters.

Before the end of 1559, Queen Elizabeth and her Parliament had settled the troublesome religious strife by providing adequate legislation for a purely national Church, a standard of discipline, a uniform and official prayer book, and a new episcopal regime sworn to uphold Supremacy, Uniformity, and the reformed condition of the Church of England. The Roman Catholic restoration was over, but Elizabeth and her advisers hoped that what remained was broad and comprehensive enough for acceptance by English subjects of all religious points of view. Henceforth, bishops were to superintend the clergy, laymen the affairs of state.

A program of anti-Roman Catholic propaganda was initiated on the popular level to secure acceptance of the queen's Settlement of Religion. The Ecclesiastical Commission could visit bishops and urge their conformity under threats of penalty and deprivation, but for the bulk of Englishmen throughout the realm, who probably were not particularly interested in ecclesiastical dispute where it did not touch them directly, a more subtle program was required. Two of these propaganda devices were especially significant: Jewel's *Apology* and the *Second Book of Homilies*.

John Jewel, bishop of Salisbury (1559-1571), published his classic *Apologia Ecclesiae Anglicanae* in 1562. It was translated into English two years later by the mother of Sir Francis Bacon as *An Apologie or answere*

*in defence of the Churche of England with a brief and plaine declaration of
the true Religion professed and used in the same.*[5] Many contemporaries accepted Jewel's *Apology* as an official statement of the Elizabethan Settlement. Some even suggested that it be taught in the universities and
placed in every parish along with the prayer book.

Bishop Jewel's *Apology* is indeed a statement of the official position
of the Church of England under Elizabeth, but it is also effective anti-
Roman Catholic propaganda. It was composed as a classic oration, setting forth those points which the apologist proposed to discuss, and at
the same time it was a pointed attack against Roman Catholic ecclesiastical administration. For example, the "Challenge" sermon begins at
a point of reference that would be sure to appeal to the ordinary citizen:
it defies antagonists of the Reformation to find evidence in either the Bible or the primitive Church that would support the excesses and innovations of the Romanist position. The old religion, now displaced in
England, robbed ordinary men of their ancient liberties through absolute tyranny and infamous corruption, Jewel argued, whereas the Reformation restored these lost liberties. Since popery was tyrannous, it
cannot have proceeded from the true Church but rather was blasphemy.
The pope hated the English merely because he missed the money which
he once extracted from them. The pope himself was the chief source of
all sedition with his weapons of excommunication, license to murder
princes by assassination, and temporal claims for jurisdiction. Indeed,
the *Apology* is a masterpiece of antipapal propaganda. The work was
sanctioned by the queen and her primates, and Elizabeth is reported to
have ordered that it be chained beside the Bible on the lectern of every
parish church.

Another effective part of the propaganda program of the Settlement
was the *Book of Homilies*.[6] Also directed toward a popular audience, it
did not attempt to deal in theological disputes as such, although it did
embody the Reformation theory. The effect of hearing these homilies
read in the churches Sunday after Sunday was undoubtedly great, par-

---

[5]For both Latin and English texts, see John Jewel, *Works* (Cambridge: The Parker
Society, 1848) 3:5-47, 52-108.

[6]The *Second Tome of Homilyes* appeared in 1563, containing twenty sermons, mainly
by Archbishop Parker. A final sermon, "An homile against disobedience and willful rebellion," was added shortly after the Northern Rebellion (1569).

ticularly since they generally complemented Jewel's vitriolics against Rome and Jewel was the author of some of the homilies. The *Homilies*, like the *Apology*, stressed England's fortunate deliverance from papal tyranny. The Church of Rome was referred to as being idolatrous,

> For shee being in deede not onely an harlot (as the Scripture calleth her) but also a foule, filthie, olde withered harlot (for she is indeede of ancient yeeres) . . . the fowlest and filthiest harlot that euer was seene . . . the great strumpet of all strumpets, the Mother of whoredome, set forth by Saint John in his Revelation. . . .[7]

According to the *Homilies*, the reformation of the Church of England had delivered Christians from such idolatry and corruption, for which all English subjects were to be grateful. Popish images were to be destroyed, according to Holy Scripture, for they were Rome's effort to sink true Christians into more idolatry.

Not only does the *Book of Homilies* attack the Church of Rome for being no true Church, but the pope's "intolerable pride" also becomes a major theme. The bishops of Rome had consistently put aside the commandments of Christ and erected their own constitutions in defiance of God's laws. For supporting evidence a long list of papal corruptions and misdeeds was catalogued. For example, Pope Gregory VII was cited for his inhumanity to Emperor Henry IV by keeping that unfortunate man freezing barefoot in the snow at Canossa.

When one considers that during this period about half of the population of England could neither read nor write and that what little was published appeared under extreme governmental and ecclesiastical censorship, one realizes that the effect of hearing these homilies directed against the pope and "his church" must have been phenomenal throughout Elizabeth's reign. When references to Romanist innovations in ecclesiastical affairs and papal corruption appear in the drama, one need not assume that playwrights had to go much farther than to the churches for such materials. Official directives insured the proper point of view. For example, Elizabeth's Injunctions of 1559 had ordered all curates of

---

[7]"An Homile Aginst perill of Idolatrie, and superfluous decking of Churches," in *Certaine Sermons or Homilies Appointed to be read in Churches, In the time of the late Queene Elizabeth of famous memory* (London: Printed by John Bill, 1623) vol. 2, ch. 2, pt. 3, p. 69.

churches to declare in sermons at least four times a year that since "all usurped and foreign power" was unscriptural, its annihilation in England was justifiable, including the destruction of "feigned miracles," relics, and images.

Meanwhile, two important developments among Roman Catholics on the Continent were taking place: the Council of Trent and the rise of the Jesuits. Following the break from Rome by several of the Continental powers, the Roman Catholic Church entered into what is commonly known as the Counter-Reformation. While the Inquisition and purges for heresy were used to secure Spain and Italy, the progressive and intellectual spirit of Humanists in the tradition of Erasmus attempted to regenerate the Church from within.

The Council of Trent was called into session to counteract the Protestant Reformation by reconsidering traditional doctrines and practices which, for the most part, had prompted the Reformation. It opened in 1545 and continued intermittently until 1563. During the third and last meeting at Trent, the Roman Catholic Church denounced the leading doctrines of Protestantism, such as individual rather than official interpretation of the Scriptures and the doctrine of justification by faith. But a positive effort was undertaken to correct the more objectionable abuses within the Church, and a more rigid discipline was proposed for the faithful. Seminaries for clerical training were ordered, but a less praiseworthy step was the approval of an index of prohibited books, to be prepared by the pope, following the example of Paul IV in 1559.

A decision of the Council of Trent called upon temporal powers of Roman Catholic Europe to recover by force those territories lost from the jurisdiction of the Roman See. As a result, France was saved from the Huguenots by massacre and bitter fighting, ten of the seventeen provinces of the Low Countries were returned to the fold, and Poland, southern Germany, and, later, Bohemia were all won back to the Roman Catholic Church. The English lived in fear of such an enterprise from France and Spain.

Another development within the Roman Catholic Church that was important in the ecclesiastical dispute in England was the rise of the Jesuits, the aggressive Society of Jesus. They became significant when certain of them were commissioned to help recover England from her alleged apostasy. By their doctrine of "probabilism," personal responsibility was lessened when a priest chose what would be the worse course if he had accepted authority for it. By invoking "mental reservation," men could often justify ignoble means toward an acceptable end. That is, if the ultimate goal was what they considered worthy, Jesuits were not bound to give the whole truth on oath to temporal officials, but rather justified their position by the doctrine of equivocation. The English regarded Jesuits not only as political subversives but as untrustworthy and unscrupulous. They were often ridiculed in stage plays of the late Settlement period.[8]

In 1568, William Allen (1532-1594), a gifted English Roman Catholic exile, founded his influential seminary at Douai to train missionary priests for England as well as to provide a theological education for English Roman Catholics. From 1579 to 1592 the college was in Rheims. In 1579 a comparable seminary was founded in Rome for English exiles. Whatever other purposes these schools may have claimed, the English understood their function to be training centers for Roman Catholic missionaries to England.

An interesting and valuable account of the English College at Rome appears in Anthony Munday's *The English Roman Life*. The English College at Rome became a center of plots against Elizabeth's government, and Jesuit missionaries were sent over under the patronage of the pope. Anthony Munday went to the Roman College for his own reasons, but when he returned to England, he became a spy for the Crown by helping to identify and arrest Jesuits as they came to England.

The Jesuits did come to England, some disguised as soldiers and artisans. They came to continue the missionary endeavor among English Romanists and others disillusioned with the Elizabethan Settlement of

---

[8]Jesuits are handled in several plays, among which are these: *The Honest Lawyer* (1615), *The Covent Garden Weeded* (before 1640) by R. Brome, and *Whore of Babylon* (1607) by Thomas Dekker. Holinshed illustrates the equivocal answers given by Jesuits when they were questioned about obedience to the queen: "If they be examined as concerning their allegiance to hir maiestie, they will make their answer after this maner; She is our lawfull souereigne ladie and queene, and we obeie hir. But then obiect vnto them, Will you obeie hir, notwithstanding the popes excommunicaton, or anie thing that he commandeth to the contrarie? Then will they answer: We desire you not to charge our consciences, and that you would not enter so deepe into our consciences, we trust the pope will not command vs anie thing against hir; and a hundred such like sleeuelesse answers they make, neuer agreeing to anie certeintie, but holding the pope in more reuerence than they do hir maiestie." Raphael Holinshed, *Chronicles of England, Scotland, and Ireland* (London: Printed for J. Johnson, et al., 1808) 4:452.

Religion. By 1580 the Jesuits had intensified their mission to recover England by sending over Robert Parsons (1546-1610) and Edmund Campion (1540-1581). Campion was arrested and executed during the next year, and Parsons fled to the Continent and enlisted the aid of William Allen in his design to bring about a Spanish invasion of England and depose Elizabeth.[9]

Pope Pius V (1566-1572) entered the dispute from a safe distance. He had written to the Duke of Alva in the Netherlands on 21 March 1569 about a possible combination of France and Spain for the purpose of invading England and deposing Elizabeth. On 3 November he wrote to both Alva and the king of Spain asking for troops to help the noble English Catholics. One might perhaps marry Mary Stuart and receive England from the hands of the pope. When this offer failed, Pius moved to relieve English Romanists from the necessity of obeying a heretical government; one may have felt that opposition to the queen was sinful. On 12 February 1570, sentence was passed by the Rota that declared Elizabeth a heretic and, consequently, her right to rule forfeit. A few days later, Pope Pius signed the famous bull *Regnans in excelsis*, and he promptly called upon France and Spain to execute the bull.

Whether the strength of *Regnans in excelsis* deterred the bulk of English recusants from their loyalty to their sovereign queen is a moot question. What is a matter of history is that the nation was fired with renewed patriotism once they felt their liberty endangered. Pius, like others before him, had not anticipated that remarkable characteristic of the English. The pope's bull excommunicating and deposing Elizabeth became an effective weapon of the queen. Religious loyalties became more political than religious at this point. Pius had unwittingly provided the legal means whereby all Roman Catholics in England could be kept under surveillance by the government as potential enemies of the state. One was forced to choose between England and Rome.[10] Pius's bull and

---

[9]Campion's trial and execution is recorded in Holinshed, 4:447-60. Campion appears in Dekker's play *Whore of Babylon* as Campeius.

[10]Holinshed expressed this point in relation to the Jesuits: "For well we know, . . . if they should denie the queenes maiestie to be their supreme princess and gouernesse in all causes: then they fall into condemnation by hir lawes. Againe, if they denied the authoritie of the pope, as of force they must needs doo, if they will esteeme themselues good subiects, and manifest a dutifull and obedient heart to hir maiestie: then they breake their vow made to the pope, and so fall into his curse and condemnation likewise: so that this is certeinlie appointed them, to cleaue faithfullie to the one, and vtterlie to forsake the other" (4:453).

the infamous St. Bartholomew's Day Massacre, two years later in France,[11] produced an understandable fear in the minds of ordinary Englishmen.[12]

After the futile effort of France to marry Elizabeth to the Duke of Anjou, the head of five provinces of the Low Countries, English Roman Catholic exiles drew up another plan, with the blessing of Pope Gregory XIII, to strike Elizabeth at three places simultaneously. The first of these was to be an invasion of Ireland, for which the pope supplied 800 Italians and Spaniards to reinforce the Spanish troops under the Earl of Desmond. This invasion, however, was easily put down in 1579 by Lord Grey de Wilton. The second part of the plan to depose Elizabeth was an attempt to revive Roman Catholicism in Scotland by support from the Guises in France. But this, too, proved futile. The third part of the program was to send subversives into England itself to work toward an opportunity to assassinate Elizabeth, or at least to work among Romanist families toward the restoration of the Roman Catholic Church in England. Working among the English in disguise, Jesuits addressed large gatherings, set up a secret printing press for the dissemination of propaganda, and distributed pamphlets throughout the realm.

After the capture of Edmund Campion in the summer of 1581, together with three Douai priests and several laymen, Parliament passed legislation "to restrain her Majesty's subjects in their due allegiance." Parliament also passed legislation that decreed that any attempt to convert English subjects to the Church of Rome or conceal Romanist missionaries was an act of high treason. Fines were levied on those who refused to attend the Church of England. A program of official espio-

---

[11]On 24 August 1572, by order of Charles IX and at the suggestion of his mother Catherine de Medici, 70,000 Huguenots, including women and children, were massacred throughout France. Pope Gregory XIII ordered a *Te Deum* in thanksgiving. Philip of Spain declared that the king of France now deserved his title of "Most Christian King," while Elizabeth in England ordered her Court into mourning and refused to receive the French ambassador.

[12]The massacre of the Huguenots was dramatized as a warning against papal policy in such plays as these: *The True and Honorable History of the Life of Sir John Oldcastle* (1599) by Munday, Drayton, Wilson, and Hathaway; *When You See Me You Know Me* (1604-1605) by William Rowley; *Devil's Charter* (1607) by Barnaby Barnes; and *Massacre at Paris* (1593) by Christopher Marlowe. However, Chapman's *The Revenge of Bussy D'Ambois* (1607-1612) causes Clermont D'Ambois to praise the Duke of Guise for his justifiable part in the Massacre, although this does not ring true for the play as a whole.

nage, answerable to Sir Francis Walsingham, was instituted to check potential threats to the queen's government.

Roman Catholics were constantly regarded with suspicion by Secretary Walsingham and his secret agents. In April 1583 Walsingham succeeded in placing a French agent in the French ambassador's household in London to spy on the ambassador. By winning over the ambassador's personal secretary, the secret agent was able to pass the ambassador's correspondence directly to Walsingham. Contained in the information thus passed to the secretary of state were the names of various Englishmen who visited the French ambassador secretly at night. One visitor was Francis Throckmorton, whom Walsingham kept under surveillance for at least six months before arresting him.[13]

Under torture, Throckmorton disclosed another plot, one which even Walsingham had not expected. He disclosed that the Duke of Guise was planning an invasion of England through Sussex in the south of England, the expense to be borne by the pope and by Spain. At the time of his arrest, Throckmorton carried a list of names of Roman Catholic nobles, along with an estimate of the troops each could muster to help the invading force.

Parliament was called into session and passed legislation to halt the threat from abroad. The Act Against Jesuits and Seminarists (1585) declared that since Jesuits had hitherto confessed that their real purpose in England had been to stir up sedition, all Jesuits were therefore banished from England. In this measure, as in other anti-Romanist legislation, the official technicality used to control offenders was not religious but political: Jesuits and seminarists were not to be persecuted for being Roman Catholics but for failing to take the Oath of Supremacy and, thereby, refusing to abide by the laws of the land as loyal subjects of Her Majesty.

It is possible, and quite likely, that Walsingham's anti-Romanist zeal led him to trump up charges against possible conspirators. Nevertheless, the accounts of conspiracies and assassins hired by the pope and Spain were passed along to the public as genuine. It is unlikely that the government's information was suspect on the popular level.

---

[13]See the details of Throckmorton's plot in Holinshed, 4:536-48.

The celebrated case of Dr. William Parry, coming close upon the heels of recent threats to the queen, became an effective instrument for government propaganda. Cecil had employed Dr. Parry, a Welshman of considerable learning, to reside abroad and act as an espionage agent against English exiles. When he returned to England, he apparently informed the Council of various attempts against the queen's life, but since the Council already knew about them no action was taken. An unexpected turn came about when Edmund Neville, an accused conspirator, implicated Parry as the instigator of a plot to assassinate Elizabeth.[14] Under torture, Parry confessed that Elizabeth's murder had been ordered by Morgan and Cardinal di Como in order to place Mary Stuart on the English throne. At his trial the state maintained that he had written to Pope Gregory for certification of his plot to murder Elizabeth and asked for papal absolution for the deed. Dr. Parry was executed for treason at Tyburn in 1585.[15]

Before the shock of Parry's cruel intention against the queen had worn from the consciousness of the nation, Walsingham "discovered" the famous Babington Plot. John Ballard, a Jesuit, was reported to have induced Anthony Babington, a young man of fortune, to join a conspiracy against the queen in favor of Mary Stuart. Babington foolishly wrote to Mary revealing the details. But the letter, like all of Mary's correspondence, first passed through Walsingham's hands. When Mary Stuart replied by consenting to the plot and spurring the participants to immediate action, she sealed her own doom. Fourteen participants in the conspiracy were executed at Tyburn in 1586.

Mary Stuart was brought to trial for her part in the conspiracy and was condemned to death. Walsingham, of course, was delighted, as was the Parliament generally. Once Mary was removed as a pawn of Roman Catholic conspirators, there would remain no Romanist pretender to the English throne. Mary Stuart was beheaded at Fortheringay Castle on 8 February 1587.

---

[14]See "A True and Plaine Declaration of the Horrible Treasons Practised by William Parrie . . . ," reproduced in Holinshed, 4:561-63.

[15]Parry's plot is used in at least two plays: Thomas Heywood's *If You Know Not Me You Know Nobody* (1603-1605), at the end of part 2, and Thomas Dekker's *Whore of Babylon* (1607).

Protestants who thought Mary Stuart's death would rid England of the succession problem were soon disillusioned when King Philip II of Spain announced himself as Mary's avenger. Before her death, Mary had formally disinherited her Protestant son in favor of Philip, and Philip claimed the English throne in his own right by descent from a marriage of John of Gaunt to a Portuguese princess.[16] The fear of Spanish domination had been kept alive in England since the time of Mary Tudor's ill-advised marriage to King Philip II. Mary Stuart's death provided him with a cause.

Pope Sixtus V (1585-1590), at a meeting with Philip on 29 July 1587, pledged a million *scudi* in gold to support the "Enterprise" against heretical England in order to replace Elizabeth with a Roman Catholic and restore the nation to papal jurisdiction. Fear swept throughout England at the news of Spanish preparations for invasion. The next year, fired with the sense of a holy crusade, the Spanish Armada sailed forth, with about 130 ships and 30,000 men, in the name of Philip and the Holy Church.

The defeat of the Armada is too well known for elaboration. Forced up the English Channel, the Spanish fleet lost several vessels in naval engagements with Charles Howard and finally fled north before severe winds. Coming off the coast of Ireland, storms ravaged other ships, and crew members were captured or killed by Irish patriots. Less than half the Armada returned to Spain.

The failure of the so-called Invincible Spanish Armada was a victory for the English and was interpreted by many Englishmen as God's judgment upon usurpers.[17] Cecil taunted the Spanish king with the fact that

---

[16]John of Gaunt's second marriage was to Constance of Castile (1372), whereby he assumed kingship of Castile and León. In an effort to claim his Spanish throne he conquered Galicia and formed an alliance with Portugal. But when his invasion of Castile ended in failure, he surrendered his claims to his daughter Catharine upon her marriage to John of Castile in 1387.

[17]The Armada is probably responsible for prompting John Lyly's *Midas* (1589-1590). It also appears as a part of Thomas Heywood's *If You Know Not Me You Know Nobody* (1603-1605) and Thomas Dekker's *Whore of Babylon* (1607). References to the Armada appear briefly in Robert Greene's *Orlando Furioso* (c. 1591), George Peele's *The Battle of Alcazar* (c. 1589), *The Famous History of the Life and Death of Captain Thomas Stukeley* (c. 1596), and Robert Greene's *The Scottish History of James the Fourth* (1589-1592). The gayest treatment appears in the song in *The Return from Parnassus* (1598-1602?).

not a Roman Catholic anywhere in England had shown any willingness to help Philip's enterprise. He even listed the names of various Roman Catholics who had performed patriotic feats during the crisis. It was a mistake to force English Roman Catholics to choose between their religion and their nation. The defeat of the Armada had the effect of drawing the people of all religious views into a spirit of national unity. Although Philip continued the war against England for as long as he lived, he never presented a serious threat to England's national security again.

The religious dispute with Rome draws to a close with Elizabeth's last anti-Romanist legislation in 1593, the Act Against Recusants. The new decade following the Armada's defeat had not brought any appreciable toleration of recusants—an important item to consider for those who attempt to make Shakespeare either a Roman Catholic or essentially sympathetic to Roman Catholics in his stage plays. The act provided that every English subject older than the age of sixteen, "being a popish recusant" and refusing to attend divine services of the Church of England, should be restricted to his place of residence and forbidden to travel more than a distance of five miles from it. If a Roman Catholic persisted in his refusal to attend the Church of England, and if he violated the act by traveling beyond the five-mile limit, he was to quit the realm.

Recusants could, however, avoid penalty if they agreed to attend the Church of England and make public submission declaring that the bishop of Rome had no legal authority over the queen of England, nor should he have had such authority. They had to further agree to obey the laws of the land as any other subject.

It is clear from this act that the queen would continue the Settlement policy employed in the religious dispute since 1559. Recusants were not persecuted for their religion; they were restrained and kept from possible conspiracy by political legislation. Punishment was for political offences against the state and not a matter of religion at all. With the kind of terror of insecurity that Roman Catholics must have experienced during those years it is inconceivable that any but the most devout could persist in recusancy.

As far as Elizabethans were concerned in the year 1593, the pope had lost his sting in England—perhaps forever. But the excitement of a century of international intrigue and the fear of invasions from Europe in the name of the Holy Church continued to fascinate English citizens for years to come. The long tradition of religious controversy between the popes and the kings of England was reflected frequently in the drama of the period. Tudor playwrights defended their own positions, often depending upon which side of the controversy the Court favored. For the majority, however, England's struggle against papal tyrany had been long-standing, reaching back to the days of William the Conqueror.

The whole religious dispute between Crown and Papacy provided playwrights with a wealth of dramatic possibilities in their efforts to placate contemporary sentiment among their audiences, whether it be through polemics, apologetics, propaganda, or sheer entertainment at the expense of one side of the controversy or the other. What really matters is that Tudor dramatists recognized in the controversy a possibility for art and relevance.

CHAPTER IV

KING JOHN
AS POLEMICAL DRAMA

The Period before 1559

The importance of early Tudor dramatists in the religious dispute with Rome should never be underestimated. During this period the stage became an effective disseminator of propaganda. Propagandists found in the drama an effective means of appealing to popular audiences by citing appropriate *exempla* of clerical corruption and exploiting their national sentiments, distrust of innovation, and fear of foreign domination.

By 1543 the interludes had become so venomously anticlerical and politically dangerous in parts that Henry's Parliament enacted its first legislation concerning the content of stage plays. Queen Mary, two weeks after entering London in 1553, issued her First Proclamation About Religion in which she absolutely prohibited unauthorized interludes. Obviously both monarchs recognized the effectiveness of drama as a polemical force in the religious dispute.

John Bale (1495-1563) was probably the most ardent propagandist for the Reformation among Tudor dramatists. Later a bishop during the reign of Edward VI, Bale had already broken with the Church of Rome by 1534 when Henry ordered the clergy to preach against the pope's usurpation in Easter Day sermons of that year. Not only did Bale respond to this, no doubt with characteristic zeal, but by 1537 his preaching in support of the Reformation had become so vehement that he was ejected from his pulpit. Thus deprived, he joined Cromwell's Company, hoping to turn the stage into an effective vehicle of propaganda for the New Faith. But when Cromwell fell from power as Vicar-General of Ecclesiastical Affairs and vicegerent in 1540, Bale fled to the Continent, where he remained an exile in Lutheran Germany until the accession of Edward VI.

King John, Bale's most valuable play, is probably the most representative polemical drama supporting the reformation of the Church of England. Although the version we now possess was revised sometime before 1561, when it may have been presented before Queen Elizabeth on her visit to Ipswich, it was first written around 1538 during Bale's tenure with Cromwell's Company. Moreover, since it incorporates much of the material that was uttered in antipapal sermons of the period, it should not be considered as drama of the period following the Elizabethan Settlement of Religion, but rather as drama of the polemical period. As such it may be seen that Bale here out-Henrys Henry.

The play itself represents a curious combination of the Morality play and the proto-Chronical play. Allegorical figures characteristic of the Moralities are brought on the stage, along with historical figures enacting scenes suggested from real events in history. However, the allegorical figures occasionally become identified with real characters. For example, the figures representing Sedition, Private Wealth, and Dissimulation as Vices occasionally assume the identities of Langton, Pandulphus, and Raymundus. Yet Bale's design, as he tells us, is not to malign the clergy, but to "vindicate a patriotic King from the Rome-inspired imputations of Polydore Vergil." King John—because he defied Rome—becomes the first great "patriot king" and the initial Reformer of the Church in England, according to the Tudor method of reading current history into the past.

As the play begins, King John, seated on his throne, tells the audience that Peter, Paul, and Jesus all teach that subjects should be obedient to their sovereign king because "true allegiance" is commendable. Since he is a king, son of a king, and grandson of an emperor, he will insure "true justice" by reforming the laws of the land and setting his subjects in good order. Widow England, having heard the opening remarks of the

king, approaches the throne and asks for the king's judgment in her
grievance against the clergy who have misused her "against all right and
justice." She describes her oppressors as

> Such lubbers as hath disguised heads in their hoods,
> Which in idleness do live by other men's goods—
> Monks, canons, and nuns, in divers colour and shape;
> Both white, black, and pied: God send their increase ill hap!   (p. 74)[1]

Sedition enters and, seeing the king and the widow alone, assumes
unwarranted familiarity by saying that he will tell tales about them,
"And say that I see you fall here to bitchery" (p. 175). John upbraids
"lewd" Sedition for his "ungodly" words in spite of Sedition's protes-
tations that he meant only to be merry. Widow England then proceeds
to air her complaint against the clergy to the king. They have taken her
possessions from her, "My woods and pastures, with other commodi-
ties" (p. 176). She denies the king's suggestion that the clergy are her
children.

> Nay, bastards they are; unnatural, by the rood!
> Since their beginning they were never good to me.
> The wild boar of Rome—God let him never to thee!—
> Like pigs they follow in fantasies, dreams and lies;
> And ever are fed with his vile ceremonies.   (p. 176)

The "wild boar of Rome," she explains, is the pope; he is a swine because "he and his to such beastliness incline."

Thus far, the theme of Bale's polemic is the corruption of the clergy.
They are indolent, avaricious, and covetous. But, unlike previous variations on this theme before the Reformation, the cause of clerical corruption is the pope. He is the progenitor of clerics who "wallow
themselves in mire" and delight in "covetous lucre." His "vile ceremonies" are no more than "fantasies." This change is the first new innovation in the polemical drama. In addition, the tone of Widow England is
bitter, hostile, and vindictive. Unlike the interludes a few years earlier,
this use of religious controversy is deadly serious.

---

[1]Page references are to the text printed in John S. Farmer, ed., *The Dramatic Writings
of John Bale* (New York: Barnes and Noble, Inc., 1966) 171–294. The lines are not
numbered.

When humor does enter, it is at the expense of the pope, and it is furnished by Sedition, the pope's friend and advocate. Sedition tells the widow to be silent, or "I shall cause the pope to curse thee as black as a crow." He then formally introduces himself: "I am Sedition, that with the Pope will hold / So long as I have a hole within my breech" (p. 177). The humor here, as in the next lines, is vulgar humor directed to the most common element of the audience. Referring to the widow, Sedition tells the king, "I will not away for that same wedred witch; / She shall rather kiss whereas it doth not itch" (p. 177).

Returning to the thesis spoken by King John at the beginning of the play, subjects are commanded by the Scriptures to obey their lawful king, Bale causes Sedition to interject the political side of England's dispute with the papacy: "Tush! the Pope ableth me to subdue both king and kaiser" (p. 177). Widow England replies to this bold statement in lines suggested by John's earlier plea for scriptural authority for a king's right to rule in his own dominions.

> Truly, of the devil they are that do any thing
> To the subduing of any Christian king;
> For, be he good or bad, he is of God's appointing:
> The good for the good; the bad is for ill doing.   (p. 177)

Both King John and Widow England have quoted scriptural proofs for the points wherein they differ from ecclesiastical policies imposed by the Church of Rome. The authority of the Scriptures for faith and conduct was, of course, one of the cardinal features of the English Reformation. Widow England's last quoted lines above are an obvious reference to Paul's Epistle to the Romans, which the Authorized Version later translated as follows:

> Let every soul be subject unto the higher powers. For there is no power but of God: the powers that be are ordained of God. Whosoever therefore resisteth the power, resisteth the ordinance of God: and they that resist shall receive to themselves damnation. For rulers are not a terror to good works, but to the evil. Wilt thou then not be afraid of the power? do that which is good, and thou shalt have praise of the same: For he is the minister of God to thee for good. But if thou do that which is evil, be afraid; for he beareth not the sword in vain: for he is the minister of God, a revenger to execute wrath upon him that doeth evil. Wherefore ye must needs be subject, not only for wrath, but also for conscience sake. (Romans 13:1-5)

Henry's argument with the papacy was largely centered upon this point. He ruled England as king by the grace of God and not by permission of the bishop of Rome. As a lawful ruler, he had scriptural authority to demand obedience from his subjects, without papal intervention or temporal jurisdiction in the king's dominions.

Widow England next explains to the king why she has been widowed: "These vile popish swine hath clean exiled my husband." She then names her husband: "Forsooth! God himself, the spouse of every sort / That seek Him in faith to the soul's health and comfort" (p. 178). Widow England explains that her husband God has been exiled out of the land because

Ye know He abideth not where His word is refused;
For God is His word, like as Saint John doth tell
In the beginning of his most blessed gospel.
The Pope's pigs may not abide this word to be heard,
Nor known of people, or had in any regard . . .   (p. 178)

Obviously the condition which Bale here describes is not the thirteenth century: it is England during the Reformation. Part of the argument of Reformers was the fact that the Bible was forbidden to lay readers. By pressing his metaphor almost beyond the limit, Bale alludes to this condition as though to say that where preaching of the Bible and lay reading are forbidden, God cannot be present.

In 1538, on the advice of Cromwell, Henry issued his Second Royal Injunctions, the second item of which ordered the entire Bible in English to be placed in each church so that the congregation might be allowed to read it. The third article declared that the Bible "is the very lively word of God, that every Christian man is bound to embrace, believe, and follow, if he look to be saved."[2] The sixth article decreed that one sermon at least once a quarter must be preached "wherein you shall purely and sincerely declare the very gospel of Christ" and urge the congregation "not to repose their trust or affiance in any other works devised by men's phantasies beside Scripture."[3]

King John promises to help the widow by calling a general assembly of nobility and clergy and placing her case before them. Sedition rebukes

---

[2] See "Second Royal Injunctions of Henry VIII," in Gee and Hardy, 275-81.

[3] Gee and Hardy, 275-81.

the king for undertaking the widow's cause and at the same time denies any kinship with England.

> Though I sometime be in England for my pastance,
> Yet was I neither born here, in Spain, nor in France;
> But under the Pope, in the holy city of Rome;
> And there will I dwell unto the day of doom.
> ....
> As I said afore; I am Sedition plain:
> In every religion and monkish sect I reign,
> Having you princes in scorn, hate, and disdain.   (p. 181)

Every congregation that belongs to the pope will know Sedition. He belongs to every religious order.

> In every estate of the clergy I play a part.
> Sometime I can be a monk in a long side cowl;
> Sometime I can be a nun, and look like an owl;
> Sometime a canon in a surplice fair and white;
> A chapterhouse monk sometime I appear in sight.
> I am our Sir John, sometime, with a new shaven crown.
> Sometime the parson, and sweep the streets with a side gown;
> Sometime the bishop with a mitre and a cope;
> A grey friar sometime with cut shoes and a rope;
> Sometime I can play the white monk, sometime the friar,
> The purgatory priest, and every man's wife desire.
> ....
> Yea, to go farther, sometime I am a cardinal;
> Yea, sometime a pope; and then am I lord of all,
> Both in heaven and earth and also in purgatory,
> And do wear three crowns when I am in my glory.   (pp. 181-182)

Henry's ostensible reason for dissolving the lesser monasteries in 1536 was to reform their "unthrifty, carnal, and abominable living."[4] Thereafter they were regarded as seedbeds of sedition.

Yet, Bale's polemic locates sedition inseparably within the Church of Rome. A common audience seeing the play in 1538, having heard at least one antipapal sermon each quarter since 1534, probably would have appreciated this scene. They would have enjoyed it not only for its jibe at the pretentious claims of papal authority ("lord of all, / Both in heaven and earth and also in purgatory"), but also for its derogation of friars and

---

[4]See "Dissolution of the Lesser Monasteries," in Gee and Hardy, 257-68.

monks who were generally unpopular and distrusted by the public. The implication that they desired "every man's wife" was by then a literary convention.

Sedition returns to his kinship with the pope and announces that he is his ambassador continually. He tells the king that he maintains traitors and rebels so that no prince can have his people's obedience, "Except it doth stand with the Pope's preeminence." But John answers firmly that his power to reign comes from God. Therefore, John says he will arrange it so that no "lewd priest" will be able to maintain Sedition any longer. Reminiscent of Henry's demands for the submission of the clergy in 1532, John declares, "We will short their horns, if God send time and space."

The troublesome question of whether an ecclesiastic has the power to depose an anointed king comes into focus when John declares that he will see to it that the clergy cannot execute their will over their lawful ruler. Sedition replies that even the king and his ecclesiastical visitors cannot be aware of the subversion taking place in the monasteries. John promises to destroy every "sect monastical" after Sedition reveals the truth about them.

> In abbeys they have so many subtle spies;
> For once in the year they have secret visitations,
> And if any prince reform their ungodly fashion,
> Then two of the monks must forth to Rome, by and by,
> With secret letters to avenge their injury.
> For a thousand pound they shrink not in such matter;
> And yet, for the time, the prince to his face they flatter.
> I am ever more their guide and their advocate.   (p. 184)

In 1535 Thomas Cromwell received his commission as vicar-general authorizing him to make a visitation to all ecclesiastical institutions throughout the realm in the name of the king. On the basis of the Visitation Commissioners' report, a formal act was passed in Parliament which dissolved the lesser monasteries the following year. In 1533 the Restraint of Appeals was enacted by Parliament, which, among other things, made it illegal to appeal a decision of the royal courts to the See of Rome.[5] The dramatic effect of these allusions must have been great

---

[5] See "Restraint of Appeals," in Gee and Hardy, 187-95.

for an audience in 1538. Henry's governmental machinery and Cromwell's zeal had exposed the latent, though sometimes active, sedition and subversion in monastic houses. While they appear to flatter the king to his face, according to the dramatist, monastics were in reality sowing sedition by secret appeals to Rome for papal intercession within the king's temporal jurisdiction. For Henry, dissolution of the seditious and allegedly immoral monasteries was inevitable if the Reformation was to succeed. If Bale was trying to provide a rationale for Henry's dissolution of the monasteries, the suggestion that subversion and sedition were rife in the monasteries was effective propaganda.

Another Romanist practice comes under attack in Bale's association of auricular confession with the work of sedition. Since the dramatist does not enter into the theological reasons for rejecting confession, he associates the objectionable practice with the pope's master design to continue his subjugation of English citizens. In this form the common audience had a reason for rejecting confession without the necessity for theological explanations. Thus Sedition tells the king that he can dwell anywhere, "In ear-confession underneath *Benedicte*; / And, when I am there, the priest may not bewray me" (p. 185). Ear-confession, Sedition says, is a secret traitor that never fails: just try to offend the Holy Church and you will find out for yourself. "For, by confession, the Holy Father knoweth / Throughout all Christendom what to his Holiness groweth" (p. 185).

When Sedition sees Nobility approaching, he tells the king that he must not be seen as he is. Therefore, he will go and disguise himself as an ecclesiastic.

> Yet, but first of all I must change mine apparel
> Unto a bishop, to maintain with my quarrel;
> To a monk or priest, or to some holy friar.
> I should never else accomplish my desire.   (p. 186)

The Morality convention of the Vice's disguising himself as Virtue was good theatre for the common audience, but here Bale no doubt uses Sedition's admission to fortify his case of a fickle Nobility, who will follow sedition when it comes in the guise of an ecclesiastic of the Old Faith and yet reject it in its proper form.

After Nobility enters, to whom the king remarks that the clergy have done great harm in departing from the Scriptures by following their own imaginations and organizing themselves into "congregations" of monks, canons, and friars, Clergy enters to pray that the king will love him as dearly as his predecessors have. When King John tells him that he will see to it that they do their duty, the clergy threaten to "seek remedy." The king then echoes the sentiments of Henry himself toward the old clergy.

> Yea, that is the cast of all your company.
> When kings correct you for your acts most ungodly,
> To the Pope, sitting in the chair of pestilence,
> Ye run to remain in your concupiscence.
> Thus set ye at nought all princely pre-eminence;
> Subduing the order of due obedience.
> But, within a while, I shall so abate your pride
> That, to your Pope, ye shall neither run nor ride;
> But ye shall be glad to seek to me, your prince,
> For all such matters as shall be within this province,
> Like as God willeth you by His Scripture evident.   (p. 189)

The Statute of Praemunire had already provided Henry with the legal right to prevent suits being carried outside the realm to the Court of Rome. This was reinforced, however, by the Restraint of Appeals (1533), which reaffirmed royal prerogatives in matters both spiritual and temporal within the realm and ordered all causes determinable by spiritual jurisdiction to be tried in royal courts without appeals to Rome. The threat of John to abate the pride of the clergy was actually accomplished by Henry when he ordered the submission of the clergy.

When Nobility tells the king that he took an oath to defend the Holy Church upon being dubbed a knight, John becomes the mouthpiece for Bale's most vitriolic attack upon the Roman Catholic Church.

> I rue it in heart that you, Nobility,
> Should thus bind yourself to the great captivity
> Of bloody Babylon, the ground and mother of whoredom—
> The Romish Church I mean—more vile than ever was Sodom;
> And, to say the truth, a meet spouse for the fiend.   (pp. 189-190)

King John then charges Clergy with abusing England.

> With your Latin hours, sermons, and poppetly plays:
> In her, more and more, God's holy word decays;
> And, them to maintain, unreasonable is the spoil
> Of her lands, her goods, and of her poor childers' toil
> Reckon first your tithes, your devotions, and your offerings,

Mortuaries, pardons, bequests, and other things;
Besides that ye catch for hallowed bells and purgatory;
For jewels, for relics, confession, and courts of bawdry;
For legacies, trentals, with scalacely masses,
Whereby ye have made the people very asses.
And, over all this, ye have brought in a rabble
Of Latin mummers, and sects deceivable,
Even to devour her and eat her up at once.   (p. 192)

The true Church, he says, is not composed of "disguised shavelings" but of "faithful hearts and charitable doings." "For when Christ's church was in her highest glory / She knew neither these sects nor their hypocrisy" (p. 192).

Thus at a sweep Bale condemns the ceremonies and rituals of the Church of Rome. Henry's First and Second Injunctions had removed many of the features mentioned above upon the justification that such practices tended toward idolatry and superstition.[6] If Bale's intention here is to condemn "popish" innovations in the Church, he resorts to reducing them to absurdity by derogatory and ridiculous qualifying phrases and words. As polemic, the scene merely reinforces the Reformation's attack upon innovation.

Bale's art is more skillfully created when he satirizes the medieval allegorization of the Scriptures. Church Fathers, such as Augustine, had used scriptural texts out of context to prove whatever point they were making. The New Learning, of course, had sought to interpret scriptural texts within their social and historical setting. John Colet, for example, gained the respect of some scholars older than himself by applying the new method to the book of Romans. Erasmus had sought to produce a Greek text of the Scriptures free from the traditional commentary that had grown up from the Vulgate. Bale introduces this part of the Reformation program by having Clergy dispute John's contention that the primitive Church did not know the great number of sects (orders) which the Church of Rome sponsors. Clergy says,

Yes, I will prove it by David substantially:
Astitit Regina a dextris tuis in vestitu
Deaurato, circumdata varietate—

---

[6]See "First Royal Injunctions" and "Second Royal Injunctions," in Gee and Hardy, 269-74, 275-81.

A queen saith David, on thy right hand, Lord, I see;
Apparelled with gold, and composed with diversity.[7]   (p. 192)

The significant point is Clergy's gloss upon the text. With total disregard for the context of the fragment, and even misunderstanding what is written, Clergy interprets it thus:

The queen is the church, which through all Christian regions
Is beautiful, decked with many holy religions—
Monks, canons, and friars, most excellent divines . . .   (p. 193)

Clergy goes on to list these "religions" in an amusing catalogue of fifty-eight separate orders of the Church. But some of them are humorous fabrications interspersed with real ones. For example, "Crucifiers, Lucifers, Bridgets, Ambrosians, / Stellifers, Ensifers, with Purgatorians, . . ." (p. 193). The effect, of course, is one of absurdity. Civil Order rightly questions Clergy's glossing of the text: "Methinketh your first text standeth nothing with your reason; / For in David's time, were no such sects of religion" (p. 194). Bale supplies King John with one of the chief complaints of Reformers against Rome's use of scriptural texts.

David meaneth virtues by the same diversity,
As, in the said psalm, it is evident to see,
And not monkish sects; but, it is ever your cast,
For your advancement, the scriptures for to wrast.   (p. 194)

A final thrust at the pope's part in the dispute over scriptural interpretation is provided by Clergy when he says that his authority for interpreting the psalm as he did comes from the pope: "Of our Holy Father, in this, I take my ground, / Which hath authority the Scriptures to expound" (p. 194).

Taken together, the passages dealing with methods of scriptural interpretation are good as Reformation propaganda. However, if one can remove from one's consciousness the polemical intent of the passages, the entire scene becomes a cleverly executed satire on the outdated, medieval use of scriptural texts associated with the Old Faith but rejected by the New.

---

[7]The Psalter in the *Book of Common Prayer* translates it thus: " . . . upon thy right hand doth stand the queen in a vesture of gold, wrought about with divers colours." Psalms 45:9.

Bale alludes to two early events in the reformation of the Church of England when he has Clergy kneel before King John. The first allusion is to the Submission of the Clergy on 15 May 1532, in which the Convocation promised not to enact any ecclesiastical policies without the king's permission.[8] The second allusion is to Henry's visit to the Convocation in 1531 when he threatened the clergy with the Statute of Praemunire. However, he promised to pardon them from forfeiture and imprisonment upon their submission to him as "Protector and Supreme Head of the English Church and Clergy."[9] Both allusions appear in the following lines. Clergy kneels and says,

> For all such forfeits as your princely majesty,
> For your own person or realm, can prove by me,
> I submit myself to you, both body and goods.   (p. 195)

To which King John replies, "Arise, Clergy, arise! and ever be obedient; / And, as God commandeth you, take us for your governor" (p. 196).

John's reference to the Scriptures is the point made in the beginning of the drama: every soul is to be subject to the governor (ruler) of the land. The fact that he becomes "Supreme Head," or as Elizabeth preferred, "governor," of the Church is but the logical extension of the Reformation's interpretation of Romans 13:1-5.

As John makes his first exit in the drama, Clergy, Nobility, and Civil Order have declared obedience to the king and have promised to have no part in sedition. But once alone, Clergy makes it clear to Nobility that he has taken the Oath of Supremacy knowing full well that the pope has the power to release him from it.

Sedition enters, and since it is he who, as the Vice, usually provides the comical element, he does not disappoint us here. Straining his neck in an effort to eavesdrop, he hears a voice saying the Litany. The Refor-

---

[8]See "Submission of the Clergy," in Henry Bettenson, ed., *Documents of the Christian Church* (New York: Oxford University Press, 1947) 308-309.

[9]Henry threatened the clergy under provisions of the Praemunire Act for having obeyed Wolsey in his capacity of papal legate. They were granted pardon from forfeiture and imprisonment upon the condition that they paid a heavy fine and recognized the king as "Protector and Supreme Head of the English Church and Clergy—*in quantum per Christi legem licet.*" Bishop Tunstall protested the ambiguity of the qualifying phrase, but Pope Clement seemed to ignore it, or at least avoided alluding to it in correspondence with Henry.

mation audience must have been delighted to hear Sedition's comment, "List, for God's passion! I trow here cometh some hogherd / Calling for his pigs. Such a noise I never heard" (p. 202). Dissimulation comes onstage, continuing his Litany. Bale, with comic irreverence, sharpens his satiric attack upon "popish" ceremony by a ridiculous parody. The humor, designed here for *reductio ad absurdum*, is enhanced by Sedition's mockery of Dissimulation's hypocritical recitation of the Litany.

Dis.: *Sancte Dominice, ora pro nobis!*
Sed.: *Sancte pyld monache*, I beshrow *vobis!*
Dis.: *Sancte Francisse, ora pro nobis!*
Sed.: Hear ye not? Cock's soul! what meaneth this
      hypocrite knave?
Dis.: *Pater noster*, I pray God bring him soon to his
      grave,
      Qui es in celis, with a vengeable *sanctificetur*,
      Or else Holy Church shall never thrive, by
      Saint Peter!   (p. 202)

Henry's First Royal Injunctions (1536) had commanded that the Lord's Prayer and the Creed should be taught in English.[10] The Second Royal Injunctions (1538) declared that whereas ecclesiastics had been accustomed "in their processions to sing *Ora pro nobis* to so many saints that they had no time to sing the good suffrages following, as *Parce nobis Domine* and *Libera nos Domine*, it must be taught and preached that better it were to omit *Ora pro nobis*, and to sing the other suffrages."[11]

Bale's Dissimulation appears ridiculous because of his hypocrisy; he prays to the saints and to God while harboring malice in his heart. Thus by a satirical parody, Bale has reinforced Henry's Injunctions and at the same time made the cleric's Litany an empty ceremony. In this case it serves as both good theatre and good polemics.

Continuing his revelation that he is responsible for meaningless externals in devotional acts, Dissimulation provides a satirical catalogue of various ecclesiastical activities.

---

[10]See "First Royal Injunctions," article 5, in Gee and Hardy, 269-74.

[11]See "Second Royal Injunctions," article 17, in Gee and Hardy, 275-81.

Then have we images of Saint Spirit and Saint Saviour—
Much is the seeking of them to get their favour:
Young women barefoot, and old men seek them breechless.
The miracles wrought there I can, in no wise, express.
We lack neither gold nor silver, girdles nor rings,
Candles nor tapers, nor other customed offerings.
Though I seem a sheep, I can play the subtle fox:
I can make Latin to bring this gear to box.
Tush! Latin is alone to bring such a matter to pass:
There is no English that can such sleights compass;
And, therefore, we will no service to be sung,
Gospel nor 'Pistle, but all in Latin tongue.   (pp. 205-206)

Bale's point, of course, is that Roman Catholics attach vain, superstitious claims to external trappings and acts of devotion which are unauthorized by the Bible. Part of the Reformation program was a clean sweep of all "superstitious" rites and forms. Since Latin was considered a necessary sacred tongue by Roman Catholic clergy, Reformers charged them with attaching miraculous claims to Latin of which plain English was incapable. The Reformation insistence upon English for the church services in England resulted in a clear statement by the framers of the Thirty-nine Articles contained in the *Book of Common Prayer*: "It is a thing plainly repugnant to the Word of God, and the custom of the Primitive Church, to have Public Prayer in the Church, or to minister the Sacraments, in a tongue not understanded of the people" (Article 24).

Bale brings onstage the four Vices for a scene of low comedy, the point of which is that the Church of Rome is corrupt because of the work of these same Vices. Although they are not the "four holy doctors" of the Church—"Austin, Ambrose, Jerome, nor Gregory"—they are the four "general proctors."

Here is, first of all, good father Dissimulation,
The first beginner of this same congregation;
Here is Private Wealth, which hath the Church infect
With all abusions, and brought it to a sinful sect.
Here is Usurped Power, that all kings doth subdue
With such authority as is neither good nor true;
And I, last of all, am even sance pere Sedition.   (p. 210)

Rejoicing in the knowledge of success, Dissimulation, Private Wealth, Usurped Power, and Sedition begin to sing. But the merry scene of song and spectacle is also a part of Bale's bitter satire on the papacy. The gist of their song is that the pope is really one of the Vices like themselves.

Private Wealth says that the "Holy Father is as good a fellow as we." That is, he continues, the Holy Father is really Usurped Power, for although the pope's apparel does not show it, "yet hath he authority / Both in heaven and earth, in purgatory and in hell." Usurped Power, representing the pope, explains his part in their revels.

> Thou knowest I must have some dalliance and play;
> For I am a man, like as another is;
> Sometime I must hunt, sometime I must Alison kiss.
> I am bold of you; I take ye for no strangers;
> We are as spiritual, I doubt in you no dangers.   (p. 211)

Dissumulation recognizes the pope as having been good to him from his childhood, and he kneels for absolution.

> For God's sake! witsave to give me your blessing here—
> A *pena et culpa*—that I may stand this day clear.
> . . . .
> And then all the devils of hell I would not fear.   (pp. 211-212)

But Usurped Power says that if Dissimulation has been guilty of preaching the gospel he cannot receive absolution. Dissimulation protests that he has never been guilty of this charge, and the pope absolves him while disguised as Usurped Power. Bale's belabored wit comes through in Sedition's comment: "A man, by the mass! cannot know you from a knave . . ."

The valuable part of this scene, in terms of Bale's polemic, is the concept of the pope as Usurped Power. Many Reformation documents contain charges against the pope's usurpation of temporal rights. For example, the First Act of Succession (1534) begins by stating that the act is mandatory because "the Bishop of Rome, and see apostolic, contrary to the great and inviolable grants of jurisdictions given by God immediately to emperors, kings, and princes, in succession to their heirs, has presumed, in times past, to invest who should please them, to inherit in other men's kingdoms and dominions."[12] Article 1 of the First Royal Injunctions (1536) ordered the clergy to observe the statutes of the realm "made for the abolishing and extirpation of the Bishop of Rome's pre-

---

[12]See "First Act of Succession," in Gee and Hardy, 232-43.

tensed and usurped power and jurisdiction within this realm." They
were also ordered to preach once every Sunday for the next quarter "that
the Bishop of Rome's usurped power and jurisdiction, having no estab-
lishment nor ground by the law of God, was of most just causes taken
away and abolished; and therefore they owe unto him no manner of obedience or subjection . . . "[13] In this scene, Bale is but echoing official
propaganda when he presents His Holiness in the guise of Usurped
Power.

Dissimulation gives messages from the clergy to Pope Usurped
Power, who begins to read them. Meanwhile, Bale continues his low
comedy between two of the Vices in the tradition of some of the Morality
plays. When Sedition repeats his surprise at discovering that the pope is
really a knave like himself, he tells Private Wealth, "I would thou hadst
kissed his arse, for that is holy." The counterplay follows.

P. W.: How dost thou prove me that his arse is holy now?
Sedit.: For it hath an hole, even fit for the nose of you!   (p. 214)

Usurped Power orders them to stop their "gauds," and he relates the
contents of his letter from the clergy.

> The bishops writeth here to me, Usurped Power,
> Desiring assistance of mine authority
> To save and support the Church's liberty.
> They report King John, to them, to be very hard,
> And to have the Church in no price nor regard.
> In his parliament he demandeth of the clergy,
> For his wars, the tent[h] of the Church's patrimony.   (p. 214)
>
> . . . .
>
> Ye know it is clean against our holy decrees
> That princes should thus contemn our liberties.
> He taketh upon him to reform the tithes and offerings,
> And intermeddleth with other spiritual things.   (pp. 214-215)

The irony of this scene is that both pope and king are apparently con-
demning each other for the same offence. That is, both appear to be
usurping the jurisdictions claimed by the other. But Bale makes it clear

---

[13]Gee and Hardy, 269-74.

how he wants the audience to respond to the complaints of the bishops against the king's meddling in affairs claimed by their respective sees.

Usurped Power adds another complaint: "Nay! besides all this, before judges temporal, / He conventeth clerks of causes criminal" (p. 215). The allusion, of course, is to Henry's policy of trying criminous clerks before temporal judges in royal law courts. Parliament's Restraint of Appeals (1533) had provided that all causes determinable by spiritual jurisdiction should be settled in royal courts of the realm, both temporal and spiritual, without appeal to Rome.

The matter of John's excommunication is dealt with at some length. The culminating factor in John's celebrated conflict with Pope Innocent III becomes apparent when Usurped Power says, "I made this fellow here the Archbishop of Canterbury, / and he will agree thereto in no condition" (p. 216). The "he" that will not agree to the pope's provision of the new archbishop of Canterbury is, of course, the historical King John. Strangely for his craft, Bale turns the allegorical figure of Sedition into Stephen Langton, the pope's choice for archbishop of Canterbury whom John refused to recognize. But, whether or not this was confusing for his audience, Bale remains constant in his thesis that Vices are responsible for the Church of Rome and its consequent usurpation of power in the English nation. According to Bale, King John had seized control of the Church in England because the pope forced Sedition upon the nation as primate. Consequently, John's actions are justifiable, and by association, so are King Henry's.

The audience is prepared for the dramatic scene of King John's excommunication by Sedition-Langton's advice to Usurped Power.

> Suspend him, and curse him, both with your word and writing.
> If that will not help, then interdict his land
> With extreme cruelness; and if that will not stand,
> Cause other princes to revenge the Church's wrong—
> It will profit you to set them a-work among.
> For clean remission, one king will subdue another;
> Yea, the child sometime will slay both father and mother.   (pp. 217-218)

Roughly, this was the case historically. Bale must have introduced this element to stir the national resentment toward foreign princes who threatened English liberties on behalf of the papacy.

When the other principals leave the stage to dress for their parts as pope, cardinal, and monk, Dissimulation addresses the audience concerning the work of that pope as Usurped Power. Among papal artifices are these: he will make such an ordinance that all humanity will be under his obedience; as God's vicar, he will advance his flock by his "politic wit"; he will create monastical orders, "monks, canons, and friars" with shaven crowns, and provide them with places "to corrupt cities and towns"; he will work miracles by the power of dead saints, images, and relics; he will institute "matins, hours, mass, and evensong" to drown out the Scriptures; he will send out pardons to save souls, and the Latin devotions with the holy rosary; he will appoint fastings and "pluck down matrimony"; he will use holy water and bread to drive away the devil; more superstition will be encouraged as he promotes blessings with black beads to help in times of evil; he will soon compel John to give up his crown because he has rebelled; he will order "Albigenes, like heretics detestable," to be burned simply because they "babble" against the Holy Father; through the preaching of Dominicans "an eighteen thousand" will be slain because they have disdained the Holy Church; and in order to do all of this he will call "a general council / Of all Christendom, to the Church of Laternense." The pope's intention shall be to suppress the gospel, yet he will "glose it" under the pretext of subduing Turks.

Bale's catalogue of historical grievances of England against the papacy is skillfully drawn. It comes at just the right psychological moment. The audience knows what is coming. John is to be humbled by the Vices disguised as religious figures. But the Reformer's suggestion of usurpation, tyranny, suppression, and bigotry is bound to create a sympathetic response on the part of the audience toward the "patriot" king. Papal demands for the very things that reformed churches had swept away creates the illusion of corruption, decadence, and medieval superstition. The fact that Dissimulation has uttered the address in praise of the papacy only tends to confirm the suspicion that the audience is hearing an exposé of fraud.

At the conclusion of Dissimulation's address, the other three return: Usurped Power is now dressed as the pope, Private Wealth is a cardinal, and Sedition is a monk. The pope chastises Dissimulation for his "liberal" exposé, and Dissimulation, falling on his knees and knocking his breast, begs absolution: "*Mea culpa, mea culpa, gravissima mea culpa!*"

The pope grants a blessing and orders him to stand aside. Then the ceremonial excommunication of King John takes place with bell, book, and candle. The pope begins the solemn ritual.

> Forasmuch as King John doth Holy Church so handle,
> Here I do curse him with cross, book, bell, and candle.
> Like as this same rood turneth now from me his face,
> So God I require to sequester him of His grace.
> As this book doth spear by my work manual,
> I will God to close up from him his benefits all.
> As this burning flame goeth from this candle in sight,
> I will God to put him from His eternal light.
> I take him from Christ, and after the sound of this bell,
> Both body and soul I give him to the devil of hell.
> I take from him baptism, with the other sacraments
> And suffrages of the Church, both Ember days and Lents.
> Here I take from him both penance and confession,
> Mass of the Five Wounds, with censing and procession
> Here I take from him holy water and holy bread,
> And never will them to stand him in any stead.   (pp. 220-221)

The effect of the scene on the Reformation audience must have been great. It contained all the elements one could desire: Vices disguised as Virtues, colorful costumes of pope and cardinal, pomp, medieval pageantry, processional, lighted tapers, stage effects of sounding bell and uplifted crosses. The Reformation audience, while no doubt impressed by the manifold allusions to rituals and "superstitious" external trappings which had not been seen in services of the New Faith for the better part of a decade, must have been struck with the seeming presumption of the Church of Rome to deal thus with an English king—be he John or Henry.

After the solemn ritual of excommunication, Bale quickly changes the mood of his play and appeals to the traditional love for spectacle onstage. This is accomplished as the Vices become merry and sing their boasts of malicious acts against King John. The pope gives instructions to the other Vices: he tells Private Wealth to take the part of Pandulphus; Stephen Langton is to be Raymundus. Then he directs Pandulphus to go through a mockery of suspending John with bell, book, and candle, but if he will not amend after that, he must lay his land under interdict and release the churches.

Stephen Langton is to command the bishops, dukes, earls, and lords to forsake the king. As Raymundus, he is to go to the Christian princes of the empire and call upon them in the pope's name to aid the Church with fire and sword. And, to Dissimulation,

> Say this to them also: Pope Innocent the Third
> Remission of sins to so many men hath granted
> As will do their best to slay him, if they may.   (p. 222)

The scene closes with the final boasting of the chief Vice. The pope will such "gear advance" that will help them all.

> First ear-confession, then pardons, then purgatory;
> Saints-worshipping then, then seeking of imagery;
> Then Latin service, with the ceremonies many,
> Whereby our bishops and abbots shall get money.
> I will make a law to burn all heretics;
> And kings to depose when they are schismatics.
> I will also raise up the four begging orders
> That they may preach lies, in all the Christian borders.
> For this and other, I will call a General Council
> To ratify them, in like strength, with the Gospel.   (p. 222)

It is a perfect ending for this highly charged scene of dramatic spectacle and song. It is the final boasting of the Vice in order to accomplish his absolute tyranny over Christendom. Yet, as polemic, it accomplishes its purpose by associating the objectionable features of Roman Catholicism with a master plan of suppression, superstition, absolutism, and hypocrisy. The boast that such things would become equated in strength with the gospel would have been intolerable to a Reformation audience. Both artistically and polemically, this scene is one of the high points of the drama.

"Actus Secundus" begins with a conversation between Sedition and Nobility in which they discuss the state of religious unrest since John's seizure of Church properties: "Canterbury monks" are exiled, bishops are reviled, and the "Cist'ian [Cistercian] monks" are in such a state of perplexity that they are also about to flee England. Sedition, who calls himself "Good Perfection," tells Nobility that Pope Innocent sends absolution, if Nobility will take the Church's part in the dispute with the king. Nobility consents and asks Sedition to put on his stole to hear his confession.

In the satirical confession and absolution which follow, Bale is careful to parody the ceremony in such a way that the pope appears to supplant Christ in the absolution: *"In nomine Domini Pape, amen!"* Nobility then begins his confession.

> I have sinned against God; I 'knowledge myself to blame—
> In the seven deadly sins I have offended sore;
> God's ten commandments I have broken evermore:
> My bodily wits I have ungodly kept:
> The works of charity, in manner, I have outslept.   (p. 226)

But Sedition, apparently unconcerned about the fact that Nobility has confessed to all the sins in the book, interrupts his confession to ask if he believes as the Holy Church teaches. He also expresses hope that Nobility flees from the "new learning." The New Learning, of course, had ushered in the Reformation, and at the same time it had divested the Church of some of its medieval security by the discovery of fraudulent manuscripts upon which many of the papacy's temporal claims were based, such as the Pseudo-Isidorian Decretals, including the Donation of Constantine. Also, as has been pointed out, the New Learning led to more accurate biblical exegesis and to higher criticism of scriptural texts. All unquestioned adherence to medieval dogmatics in philosophy, theology, and science, for the most part, set themselves in opposition to the New Learning of the Renaissance. Nobility, then, may speak more accurately than Bale realized when he answers, "From the new learning? Marry, God of heaven save me! / I never loved it of a child, so mote I thee" (p. 226).

When Sedition continues to catechize his suppliant concerning the creed, the Latin "Ave Mary," "dirge," "seven psalms and litany," belief in purgatory, and holy bread, Nobility gives all the right responses. Then he asks for papal absolution, but Sedition withholds it, while he has him under *"benedicte,"* until he will agree to carry out the pope's wishes.

> The Pope willeth you to do the best ye can
> To his [John's] subduing for his cruel tyranny;
> And, for that purpose, this privilege graciously
> Of clean remission he hath sent you this time,
> Clean to release you of all your sin and crime.   (p. 227)

Bale's polemics at this point, of course, are centered about the theological aspects of the forgiveness of sin. Whereas the process of absolution would have involved contrition, confession, and penance (satisfaction) for the penitent, Sedition apparently equates penance with the pope's personal will. Consequently, Sedition, in his role as priest, withholds absolution until the pope's interests have been fulfilled by the penitent to the satisfaction of the priest. Protestant theology would have insisted upon justification by faith and not by works of sacramental penance. In this instance, Bale is discrediting the whole institution of absolution by revealing an abuse of the rite that even Roman Catholics would have denounced. Bale would have insisted that forgiveness not be denied to a sincere penitent based on any conditional works.

Nobility, however, hesitates to rebel against the king, for his "princely estate and power is of God." Bale, of course, here returns to his recurring theme which was stated by the king himself at the beginning of the play. Sedition reminds Nobility that "God's vicar" has given him full authorization for rebelling against the king, and if he does not obey the pope, Nobility will fall "in danger of damnation." Finally, Nobility agrees to obey the pope's demands for a conspiracy against King John. Sedition then completes the ritual of absolution.

> I assoil thee here from the King's obedience,
> By the authority of the Pope's magnificence.
> *Auctoritate Roma in pontificis ego absolvo te*
> From all possessions given to the spiritualty,
> *In nomine Domini Pape, amen!*
> Keep all things secret, I pray you heartily.   (p. 227)

Bale's satirical confession and absolution scene ends with Nobility's coalition in treason against the king.

An interesting point of church and state relationship has been raised for the consideration of the audience: If the Bible clearly commands absolute obedience to the king as God's anointed minister for good or for evil, does the papacy have scriptural authority to command royal subjects to rebel against their lawful king? An English Reformation audience would have known the answer without a doubt. Bale's polemics, then, have been served in this scene by making the pope the instigator of treason—against scriptural authority. The political nature of ecclesiastical controversy has become apparent again.

In the next scene, Sedition, as Archbishop of Canterbury Stephen Langton, is welcomed into the realm by Civil Order and Clergy. Civil Order laments the state of religious discord between his friend Clergy and King John: "Right sorry I am of the great controversy / Between him and the king, if I might it remedy" (p. 228). Sedition-Langton tells the others that he is authorized to lay the king's dominions under interdict, and he produces papal bulls to prove it. Clergy, having prayed for the pope's "holy majesty," is commanded to "sit down on your knees" and receive absolution, "*A pena et culpa*, with a thousand days of pardon."

At this point, Bale introduces a theological subtlety in the doctrine of penance which may have been lost on his general audience. Since the time of Richard of St. Victor in the twelfth century, Roman Catholic theologians had insisted upon the distinction between *poena* and *culpa* in the sacrament of penance. That distinction was reconfirmed in the Canons of the Council of Trent: the penitent's *culpa* is remitted by the words of absolution, as are the consequences of sin, but the *poena* remains and must be satisfied by some equivalent temporal punishment to placate the eternal justice of God. Bale disregards this distinction between *poena* and *culpa* and causes Sedition-Langton to promise absolution from both *culpa* and *poena*, seemingly without the necessity for *poena*. The dramatist as polemicist has thus succeeded in "exposing" absolution as fraudulent and as an instrument of the papacy to be used against princes in their own dominions.

The scene quickly moves into another attempt at humor when the Vice Sedition-Langton exhibits a catalogue of holy relics.

Here is first a bone of the blessed Trinity,
A dram of the turd of sweet Saint Barnaby.
Here is a feather of good Saint Michael's wing,
A tooth of Saint Twyde, a piece of David's harp string,
The good blood of Hales, and our blessed Lady's milk;
A louse of Saint Francis in this same crimson silk.
A scab of Saint Job, a nail of Adam's toe,
A maggot of Moses, with a fart of Saint Fandigo.
Here is a fig-leaf and a grape of Noe's vineyard,
A bead of Saint Blythe, with the bracelet of a bearward.
The devil that was hatched in Master John Shorn's boot,
That the tree of Jesse did pluck up by the root.
Here is the latchet of sweet Saint Thomas' shoe,
A rib of Saint Rabart, with the huckle bone of a Jew;

Here is a joint of Darvel Gathiron,
Besides other bones and relics many one.   (p. 229)

It is low humor, and it is effective for the same reason that Heywood's
and Erasmus's catalogues of relics are effective: it reduces to absurdity
the pretentious claims made by those who sought some personal motive
in exhibiting false relics.

But for Bale's audience, the absurdity attaches itself to the Roman
Catholic Church which venerated pilgrimages and holy relics and insisted upon their employment in devotional works. Both of Henry's
Royal Injunctions had condemned the use of feigned images and relics,
"kissing or licking the same," and preachers who had extolled feigned
relics "or any such superstition" were ordered to recant and preach to
their congregations that there was no scriptural authority permitting
such. As polemic, the catalogue helps associate the medieval church
with superstition and fraud.

Sedition completes the ritual of absolution, "*In nomine Domini Pape,
amen!*," and orders the "penitents" to rise. Now that they are clean, he
says, they are likely to have an increase of children, cattle, and corn. Bale
continues his low comedy by a traditional allusion to clerical unchastity.
When Civil Order reminds him that clergy can have no children, Sedition, who is consistently the humor device, answers, "Tush! though he
has none at home, he may have some abroad" (p. 230).

Returning to his program of conspiracy against the king, Sedition
tells Clergy what he must do for the pope and the Holy Church. He is to
stir up the king's subjects: "Let them show King John no more favour
than a Turk; / Everywhere stir them to make an insurrection" (p. 230).
Clergy agrees to this and suggests that he can lament the interdiction in
his sermons and tell the people that they are in danger of eternal damnation as a result. Moreover, he continues, he will incite the people to
force John's abdication by closing the church doors, silencing church
bells, withholding the Eucharist, and denying burial and baptism—actions listed in Innocent's actual interdict. Civil Order offers to provoke
"the great men" of the realm to take "common's part" in the controversy,
for "if the Church thrive, then do we lawyers thrive." When they hear
King John approaching, the Vices run offstage to hide.

John, apparently addressing the audience directly rather than en-
gaging in soliloquy, complains that the clergy are allied against him sim-

ply because he has attempted to "correct all vice" by enforcing justice upon all transgressors.

> And because I will not be partial in mine office
> For theft and murder, to persons spiritual,
> I have against me the priests and the bishops all.   (p. 232)

He then alludes to his father's own difficulties with the criminous clerks during his reign.

> A like displeasure in my father's time did fall,
> Forty years ago, for punishment of a clerk:
> No counsel might them to reformation call,
> In their opinion they were so sturdy and stark,
> But against their prince to the Pope they did so bark,
> That here, in England, in every city and town
> Excommunications as thunderbolts came down.
> For this their captain had a ster-apared crown,
> And died upon it without the king's consent.
> Then interdictions were sent from the Pope's renown,
> Which never left him till he was penitent,
> And fully agreed unto the Pope's appointment,
> In England to stand with the Church's liberty;
> And suffer the priests to Rome for appeals to flee.
> . . . .
> Since my father's time I have borne them grudge, therefore,
> Considering the pride and the captious disdain
> That they have to kings which ought over them to reign.   (p. 232)

John's speech is effective propaganda for the Reformation audience because it helps create sympathy for the king in his just cause against a corrupt and privileged clergy. Bale's polemical intent places John's dispute with the clergy in what he saw as a continuing struggle for all English kings who have attempted to punish criminous clerks. The reference here to the well-known case of Henry II and his controversy with Becket was a skillful maneuver on Bale's part. As has been observed earlier, Henry's Second Royal Injunctions (1538) had removed Becket's fast day from the Church calendar. During that same year the monastery at Canterbury was dissolved, Becket was tried for treason posthumously, his bones were disinterred and burned publicly, and his name was removed from the service books.

Bale's allusion to Becket's defiance of Henry II probably came while the Royal Injunctions and the suppression of Becket's shrine were still fresh in the minds of the audience. Thus, Bale implies in his antipapal propaganda that the Roman Catholic clergy have always been responsible for treason in England. Artistically, the "soliloquy" is effective, since it reveals John's sense of justice, patriotism, and equity before he becomes the helpless victim of a grand conspiracy. He expresses the point that most of the other kings engaged in the ecclesiastical controversy had made: kings should rule priests; priests should not rule kings.

Private Wealth, dressed as cardinal, comes onstage and bears a message to the king from the Holy Father: John is to make full restitution for Church properties seized during the interdict, he is to receive Stephen Langton as primate, monks in exile are to be returned to their houses, and the king is to restore all that he has "ravished" from the Holy Church "and more." John declares that he is willing to adhere to all of the pope's demands, except for receiving Langton because Langton is "inclined to sturdiness and sedition." Yet, if the man will promise "new behaviour," John will allow him some other benefice in the kingdom. Private Wealth tells the obstinate king that the Holy Church does not so deal with her prelates, but rather she administers punishment to the disobedient kings and princes.

Bale is moved to reiterate his recurring thesis to the effect that Christian kings rule by the grace of God and not by permission of the papacy.

> The power of princes is given from God above;
> And, as saith Solomon, their hearts the Lord doth move.
> God speaketh in their lips when they give judgment;
> The laws that they make are by the Lord's appointment.
> Christ willed not his the princes to correct,
> But to their precepts rather to be subject.
> The office of you is not to bear the sword,
> But to give counsel according to God's word.   (p. 234)
> ....
> I cannot perceive but ye are become Bel's priests,
> Living by idols; yea, the very Antichrists!   (p. 235)

It is a clear statement defining the root problem of the religious dispute: temporal jurisdiction of the papacy within a king's dominion is contrary to the spiritual ideal. By implication, Bale is playing upon this theme to justify the frequent Reformation charge that temporal claims of the papacy were usurpations of English royal prerogatives. Therefore, the function of the clergy should be spiritual, not temporal, and clerics should be bound by the laws of the land to the same degree that all other English subjects are bound.

At the king's tirade against Clergy, Private Wealth executes the papal bulls of excommunication and interdiction.

> Here I curse you for the wrongs that ye have done
> Unto Holy Church, with cross, book, bell, and candle;
> And besides all this, I must you otherwise handle.
> Of contumacy the Pope hath you convict:
> From this day forward your land stand interdict.   (p. 235)

Bishops throughout Christendom are ordered to suspend anyone who seeks to give aid, and subjects are absolved from oaths of obedience.

Bale's appeal to the national consciousness of the English and their love for independence from foreign domination could have no better opportunity than that afforded by this scene. The question of the pope's authority to depose divinely anointed kings was still in the background, but the audience in 1538 had probably read for the first time Pope Paul III's bull *Eius qui immobilis* (issued 30 August 1535), deposing Henry, excommunicating him, and laying England under interdict. Psychologically, the insertion of this material was powerful propaganda. What had happened to poor King John had now happened to poor King Henry The enemy in both cases is the same: the usurping papacy.

Just then the alarm is sounded announcing a foreign invasion of England. King John rebukes Private Wealth and asks him if this is what the Holy Church means by charity. Answering his own question, he denies that such procedure could come from God, rather it proceeds from the devil. Since Private Wealth forbids preaching of the gospel, Henry continues, he also forbids the "opening" of the Scriptures, for "it standeth not to your advantage." But Private Wealth responds with another possible allusion to *Eius qui immobilis*.

> Ah! now I tell you, for this heretical language
> I think neither you, nor any of yours, I wis—
> We will so provide—shall wear the crown after this.   (p. 236)

Obviously, Bale sees John's controversy with the papacy and the clergy as a matter of politics in which Rome presumes to depose kings and deny royal prerogatives in defiance of the Scriptures.

King John asks Clergy to explain what biblical authority entitles the papacy thus to excommunicate anyone: "Prove it by Scripture, and then will I it allow—" (p. 238). And assuming that Clergy is unable to answer, John reduces the effect of papal excommunication to a meaningless curse: "But this know I well: when Balaam gave the curse / Upon God's people they were never a whit the worse" (p. 238).

Clergy makes it clear that scriptural precedent is unimportant: what counts is papal authority. Consequently, Nobility demonstrates his preference for the papacy above God's anointed king and hence above God himself whenever he is forced to make a clear choice.

> I shall desire you, as now, to pardon me:
> I had much rather do against God, verily!
> Than to Holy Church to do any injury.   (p. 239)

Bale restates the whole Reformation program in these lines:

> His [Commonalty's] outward blindness is but a signification
> Of blindness in soul, for lack of information
> In the word of God; which is the original ground
> Of disobedience, which all realms doth confound.
> If your grace would cause God's word to be taught sincerely,
> And subdue those priests that will not preach it truly,
> The people should know to their prince their lawful duty;
> But, if ye permit continuance of hypocrisy
> In monks, canons, and priests, and ministers of the clergy,
> Your realm shall never be without much traitory.   (p. 245)

The program outlined here is precisely Henry's program of reformation, beginning with the clergy. Not only did Henry order that the English translation of the Bible be read in churches, but he also ordered regular preaching of the gospel. Preachers were required to take the Oath of Supremacy, or, if they resisted, they would incur the penalty of treason.

Cardinal Pandulphus comes onstage and rebukes blind Commonalty for having obeyed King John, whereupon he submits himself as a repentant figure: "*Peccavi, mea culpa!* I submit to your holiness." When the cardinal reports that "French King Philippe" is invading the land in order to subdue "this heretic," Commonalty exits with the mere excuse, "I must needs obey when Holy Church commandeth me."

Cardinal Pandulphus orders Widow England to desert the king, but she loyally remonstrates, "I will not away from mine own lawful king, / Appointed of God, till death shall us depart" (p. 247). Widow England says that she already suffers from Rome's "subtle practice,"

And am clean undone by your false merchandise,
Your pardons, your bulls, your purgatory pick-purse,
Your Lent fasts, your shrifts, that I pray God give you his curse!   (p. 247)

But, replies Pandulphus, she will "smart" more, for great navies are on
their way at this very hour to fight with "this Loller here" in the name
of the Holy Church: the French will attack from the south and burn their
way to London Tower; Spanish ships "full of gunpowder" (in 1212!) will
come from the west; the Scots will press down with land armies from the
north; and "Esterlings, Danes, and Norways" will land in the east. Sedition promises eternal salvation to those who take part in the crusade
against King John.

To all that will fight I proclaim a jubilee
Of clean remission, this tyrant here to slee;
Destroy his people, burn up both city and town,
That the Pope of Rome may have his sceptre and crown!
In the Church's cause to die, this day, be bold:
Your souls shall to heaven ere your flesh and bones be cold.   (p. 248)

Dramatically the scene is good. It pictures John in the final throes of
his dilemma. All except enfeebled England have deserted him, and the
Vice as cardinal taunts him with news of a holy crusade against the heretical king. Polemically the scene is effective in sustaining sympathy for
a patriotic king unjustly abused by the clergy, nobility, and commonalty.

John exits for a brief consultation with inconstant Nobility before
surrendering to the cardinal, and Sedition gloats over his forthcoming
victory. Bale uses this brief scene to reinforce the corrupt motivation behind the pope's crusade.

Our Holy Father may now live at his pleasure,
And have habundaunce of wenches, wines, and treasure.
He is now able to keep down Christ and His Gospel,
True faith to exile, and all virtues to expel.
Now shall we ruffle it in velvets, gold, and silk;
With shaven crowns, side-gowns, and rochets white as milk.   (p. 250)

And the fact that Sedition can hardly control himself for laughing so
hard at the king's plight would doubtless have the same effect upon the
audience that any triumphant laughter by the Vice would have had in
Morality plays.

John's submission comes quickly. He returns to the scene and sol-
emnly announces that should he continue the reformation, his subjects
would merely suffer at the hands of foreign invaders. Since the thoughts
of shedding Christian blood and the inevitable ravening of innocent vic-
tims are repugnant to the king, he yields to his more powerful adversary:
"These things considered, I am compelled this hour / To resign up here
both crown and regal power" (p. 251). For, he says as he considers England's remonstrance, he would rather give up his crown than have his
people suffer. Therefore, "Here I submit me to Pope Innocent the
Third, / Desiring mercy of his Holy Fatherhood" (p. 252). Removing
his crown and handing it to the cardinal, John announces his abdication
and submission to Rome.

> To him I resign here the sceptre and the crown
> Of England and Ireland, with the power and renown,
> And put me wholly to his merciful ordinance.   (p. 252)

Cardinal Pandulphus triumphantly tells John that he will keep the
crown for the pope until such time as the ex-king pledges himself and
his heirs to receive the crown from the pope and make the kingdom a
papal fief ("fe[off]-farm"). Moreover, he must agree to pay a token of "a
thousand mark" annually, in addition to the Peter's pence, and to give
"three thousand mark" to the archbishop of Canterbury for his injuries.
He must also pay "forty thousand mark" in restitution to the Church for
seizure of her properties. The clergy, however, are not to be taxed. England probably expressed the sentiment of the audience at this point
when she says, "So noble a realm to stand tributary, alas, / To the devil's
vicar! such fortune never was!" (p. 253).

Treason comes onstage and explains that his work is now complete,
for he has seduced Nobility to treason while withholding absolution
from him until he consented. Henceforth, no priest will ever obey God's
word or the gospel.

> In the place of Christ I have set up superstitions;
> For preachings, ceremonies; for God's word, men's traditions.
> Come to the temple and there Christ hath no place;
> Moses and the pagans doth utterly him deface!   (p. 255)

The audience is left to assume that Roman Catholics have substituted the
religion of mankind for the religion of Christ and His word. The point

that Rome prefers the ancient rituals of the Old Testament Church to the
pristine purity of the New Testament Church is further elaborated by
Treason when he explains what they have retained from Moses.

> All your ceremonies, your copes, and your censers, doubtless;
> Your fires, your waters, your oils, your altars, your ashes,
> Your candlesticks, your cruets, your salt, with such like trashes—
> Ye lack but the blood of a goat, or else a calf.
> ....
> Of the pagans ye have your gilded images all,
> In your necessities upon them for to call;
> With crouchings, with kissings, and setting up of lights,
> Bearing them in procession, and fastings upon their nights;
> Some for the toothache, Some for the pestilence and pox;
> With images of wax to bring money to the box.   (pp. 255-256)

Bale's polemical intent is a conscious effort to equate Roman Catholic ritual with ancient Hebraic customs and ceremonies, which, according to Reformation theologians, have no signification in a New
Testament Church. Treason tries a final thrust at retaining unscriptural
ceremonies in the Church of Rome.

> It is the living of my whole congregation.
> If superstitions and ceremonies from us fall,
> Farewell monk and canon, priest, friar, bishop, and all!   (p. 256)

All we have retained from the Church of Christ, explains Treason, are
the "epistle and the gospel," but they are in Latin so that no man shall
be able to understand them.

Pandulphus finally lifts the interdict from England and commands
the king to meddle no more in the Church's affairs nor forbid appeals to
Rome. Since the pope has blessed the nation again, everything will pros-
per. But, of course, the gospel is not to be preached. When John leaves
the stage, Sedition reveals that the king will now become their slave by
slaying their enemies and burning "such as believe in Christ." Yet, just
to make sure, they decide to encourage Philip of France's invasion of
England.

Dissimulation enters and, after receiving Sedition's absolution, tells
him of a plan for poisoning the king. He will share a drink with John and
put the venom in his glass. Even if he should die in the effort, continues
Dissimulation, the monks would pray for his soul "so bitterly" that he
would not go to hell or purgatory. If the priests "grunt a good pace *pla-*

cebo with requiem mass," he shall be ushered directly to Paradise. Sedition tells him to order five monks at Swinsett Abbey to sing for his soul "so long as the world is during." Hearing the king's approach, Sedition completes the absolution, "*Ego absolvo te in nomine Papae, amen!*" and the Vices exit.

King John laments his sad estate.

> . . . My sceptre I gave up lately
> To the Pope of Rome, which hath no title good
> Of jurisdiction; but of usurpation only[.]   (p. 266)

But even so, the French forces under Philip's son Louis continue their invasion of the realm. John says that the pope and his priests are "poisoners" of all lands, and he sounds a warning to the public: "All Christian people, beware of traitorous priests! / For, of truth, they are pernicious Antichrists" (p. 267).

Disguised as Simon of Swinsett, Dissimulation enters and declares his love for the king. Under pretense of fidelity and amity, he gives the poisoned cup to the king, but John makes him drink half of the potion first. Going aside to Sedition, Dissimulation says that he is dying.

> To send me to heaven go ring the holy bell,
> And sing for my soul a mass of Scala Coeli,
> That I may climb up aloft with Enoch and Heli—
> I do not doubt it but I shall be a saint.
> Provide a gilder mine image for to paint;
> I die for the Church with Thomas of Canterbury—
> Ye shall fast my vigil, and upon my day be merry.
> No doubt but I shall do miracles in a while;
> And therefore, let me be shrined in the north aisle.   (p. 269)

The scene is comically satirical of the Roman Catholic veneration of saints. It is deliberate humor provided by the Vice, but it comes at a rather awkward place dramatically because the king is also dying. The Reformation audience must have felt some relief in the comical destruction of at least one of the Vices. By associating Dissimulation with Becket, the audience would gain some degree of satisfaction from knowing how short-lived was the veneration of such "traitorous" martyrs in England. Royal Injunctions, of course, had prohibited feigned miracles of saints and the depiction of such miracles on stained glass church windows.

Once the king is dead, Verity enters, accompanied by Nobility, Clergy, and Civil Order, and assures the audience that regardless of what chroniclers have written about the king, John was "both valiant and godly." What "Polydorus" (Polydore Vergil) wrote about him was at the suggestion of the "malicious clergy." By quoting scriptural texts, Verity rebukes Nobility, Clergy, and Civil Order for abusing their lawful king: they "call to God in vain" who hold their princes "in disdain."

Imperial Majesty (representing King Henry VIII) enters and asks Verity if he has done everything he was instructed to do. Verity replies affirmatively and tells the Vices to kneel and ask the king's pardon for their treatment of King John. Each in his turn kneels and declares solemn allegiance after first begging pardon. Imperial Majesty says that so long as he lives, "popish prelates" will do no injury to Verity in England. Bale cannot resist repeating his theses—this time in the words of Verity himself.

> For God's sake obey, like as doth you befall;
> For, in his own realm, a king is judge over all
> By God's appointment; and none may him judge again
> But the Lord Himself: in this the Scripture is plain.
> He that condemneth a king, condemneth God, without doubt;
> He that harmeth a king, to harm God goeth about.
> He that a prince resisteth, doth damn God's ordinance;
> And resisteth God in withdrawing his affiance.
> All subjects offending are under the king's judgment:
> A king is reserved to the Lord omnipotent.   (p. 278)

Imperial Majesty thus completes his case against papal interference within a king's dominions. But since the papacy is not content to restrict its jurisdiction to matters spiritual, Verity's speech seems directed to the important point of his breach with Rome.

> I charge you, therefore, as God hath charge[d] me,
>   To give to your king his due supremity;
> And exile the Pope this realm for evermore.   (p. 279)

For, although they do not realize it, even popes should obey the biblical injunction to be obedient to temporal rulers.

Clergy replies that they will exile the pope from the realm, and he tells Imperial Majesty, "your grace shall be the supreme head of the

Church." Nobility declares that the pope is "worse than a Turk," who works through tyranny.

> This bloody butcher, with his pernicious bait,
> Oppress Christian princes by fraud, craft, and deceit,
> Till he compel them to kiss his pestilent feet,
> Like a leviathan sitting in Moses' seat.   (p. 281)

The pope, he continues, is the "beast and slaughterman of the devil"—a "Babylon boar." Civil Order joins the general antipapal declarations by saying,

> I think he hath sprung out of the bottomless pit;
> And, in men's conscience, in the stead of God doth sit;
> Blowing forth a swarm of grasshoppers and flies—
> Monks, friars, and priests—that all truth putrefies.   (p. 281)

When the principals have declared their allegiance to the Supreme Head, Imperial Majesty charges them "to regard the word of God over all" and to accept it as the sole truth and rule. Clergy promises to exile Usurped Power and to defend the king's "supremacy," Nobility promises to cast out Private Wealth from the monasteries, and Civil Order promises to hang Dissimulation in Smithfield along with his superstition.

As the triumphant note resounds onstage, Sedition, the most vicious Vice, enters singing in characteristic jocularity. The drama is now at its highest peak: poor King John has been revenged, the fickle subjects have repented and sworn oaths of allegiance to Imperial Majesty, the papacy has been put out of England, and now Bale moves to dispose of Sedition, to the great delight of the audience. Yet the treatment is comical.

When Imperial Majesty calls upon him to give an account of himself, the Vice pleads for sanctuary: "A sanct'ary! a sanct'ary! for God's dear passion, a sanct'ary! / Is there none will hold me? and I have made so many!" (p. 284). But pleading in vain he says, "I am windless, good man! I have much pain to blow."

Evading the question of his identity consistently, Sedition says that his godmother called him Holy Perfection. The others onstage, however, identify him as Sedition, although he denies it. But when Clergy, Nobility, and Civil Order have again identified him as the chief Vice, Sedition promises to tell the truth, past and future, if they will agree to pardon him.

The conversation that follows Imperial Majesty's pardon of the Vice helps expose the channels through which much of Sedition's work was accomplished.

> Sed.: I will tell to you such treason as ensueth—
>   Yet a ghostly father ought not to bewray confession.
> I. M.: No confession is but ought to discover treason.
> Sed.: I think it may keep all thing, save heresy.
> I. M.: It may hold no treason, I tell thee verily!   (p. 285)

Bale alludes to Henry's Royal Injunctions again when Sedition says,

> Ye gave injunctions that God's word might be taught;
> But who observe them? full many a time have I laught
> To see the conveyance that prelates and priests can find.   (p. 286)

He continues, if the people could know the Bible, they would then accept no head but their prince. Alluding to Parliament's Reformation legislation and the need for strict enforcement, Bale causes Sedition to boast,

> In your parliament, command you what you will,
> The Pope's ceremonies shall drown the Gospel still.
> Some of the bishops at your injunctions sleep;
> Some laugh and go by; and some can play bo-peep.
> Some of them do nought but search for heretics
> Whilst their priests abroad do play the schismatics.   (p. 286)

As part of his antipapal propaganda, Bale uses Sedition's confession to demonstrate that the work of the Reformation is not yet complete: the clergy are still lax in their duty. A natural response from the Reformation audience would be, "Compel the prelates to conform!" This, of course, would be compatible with Bale's purpose. The point is reinforced when Sedition confesses that he is but waiting for the opportunity to reinstate the pope's jurisdiction in England. As he says, the pope is a "jolly fellow."

But Sedition's own confession condemns him. He has revealed that he really seeks to ruin Imperial Majesty, just as he did King John. Imperial Majesty orders Sedition to be drawn to Tyburn, hanged, and quartered. His head is to be placed on London Bridge for public scrutiny. The Vice's plea is intentionally and ironically humorous.

> Some man can tell the Pope, I beseech ye, with all my heart:
> How I am ordered for taking the Church's part,
> That I may be put in the holy litany
> With Thomas Becket, for I think I am as worthy.
> Pray to me with candles, for I am a saint already.
> O blessed Saint Patrick! I see thee, I verily!   (pp.289-290)

And lest his audience should miss the connection, Bale explains it when Imperial Majesty says,

> King John ye subdued, for that he punished treason,
> Rape, theft and murder, in the holy spiritualty:
> But Thomas Becket ye exalted without reason,
> Because that he died for the Church's wanton liberty,
> That the priests might do all kinds of iniquity,
> And be unpunished. . . .   (p. 290)

After Imperial Majesty's exit, the three principals summarize Roman Catholic techniques for domination of the Church of England. Nobility explains to the audience that "Antichrist's whelps" abuse royal and noble princes to further their schemes. Actions they have seen onstage demonstrate how Romanists have defiled the law and blinded Nobility through "prodigious lies," "crafts uncomely," and "mischief" against "nature, manhood, and grace."

Clergy explains that their "masses" and "foundations" are designed to poison their king; confession surpasses all other means of treason; they can make saints of the worst knaves in order to promote their economy; they invest their saints with miraculous powers to help their market; and whoever maligns one of their saints is damned to hell without remedy. Civil Order says that the audience has seen what results from sedition as it preys upon the superstitious. Therefore, it is expedient to beware of sedition in its devious forms.

Bale's polemic has made Henry VIII a male Nemesis to rectify the wrongs done to King John during his dispute with the pope. Through his own crusade against a corrupt and treasonous clergy, Henry rises above the tragedy of good King John and becomes the agent of God's vengeance against the wicked powers of Antichrist. Such a device gives the Reformation audience a feeling that justice has been done, though long overdue. The Vices are exiled, the sinners are repentant, and the chief Vice has gone to Tyburn where all traitors go. A final summary of "popish" devices serves the cause of Bale's propaganda. The audience must be thoroughly convinced that the tyranny of Rome can come again to England, if the clergy are not brought into conformity to the Reformation program. The final scene is effective polemics as well as good art.

The drama as a whole provides a rationale for the English Reformation under Henry VIII. The play's effectiveness lies in its propaganda for a popular audience. Its polemics are geared away from theological disputations and toward a general condemnation of "popish" innovations, tyranny, hypocrisy, fraud, greed, and murder in a corrupt religious system.

By depicting John as a national patriot defeated by the powers of Antichrist and a corrupt clergy, Bale gave his audience an exciting *exemplum* of what happens when English subjects obey humans rather than the word of God. Dramatically, the play is crude, rambling, poorly constructed, often tedious, and better considered in the tradition of Morality plays. Yet, it contains all the elements that would appeal to an early sixteenth century audience.

It is remarkable, however, that Bale constructed a lengthy drama almost entirely out of the heated issues of the religious controversy taking place in his own day. With more matter and less art, Bale produced a timely and relevant tract supporting official documents of the English Reformation in its first phase.

CHAPTER V

REPRESENTATIVE DRAMA
OF THE
ELIZABETHAN SETTLEMENT

The Period after 1559

The polemical drama of the English Reformation may seem to suffer from too much propaganda and not enough self conscious art on the part of the dramatists. However, stage plays written after the Elizabethan Settlement of Religion reveal an effective use of these controversial materials in the creation of some of the world's finest literature. When it became apparent that the Reformation would continue to safeguard the English national Church from papal control, dramatists no longer felt the necessity for polemics in the same way Bale and others had.

But the old hostility did not disappear after 1559. On the contrary, some of the most vitriolic abuses of the papacy and of the Roman Catholic ecclesiastical system continued to appear in the works of playwrights like Marlowe and Dekker. For the most part, however, derogatory and hostile allusions to Roman Catholics were prompted by the continuing fear throughout Elizabeth's reign that the papacy would again endeavor to reclaim the Church of England through the use of foreign invasions by loyal powers on the Continent. Spain's Philip II, for example, saw himself as the temporal arm of the papacy, destined to reclaim territories lost to "heretics" in the name of the Holy Church. His celebrated Armada is evidence of how seriously he took his mission. Spain and Spanish clerics in the drama of the period often became synonymous with the Roman Catholic Church's continuing endeavors to usurp ancient royal prerogatives in England.

The Elizabethan Settlement of Religion was perhaps the most decisive event in the ecclesiastical controversy. Indeed, it established the supremacy of the Protestant theory in England and determined the course the Church would follow for the remainder of Elizabeth's reign.

The machinations of Rome in attempting to depose Elizabeth and reclaim England for the pope provided dramatists with some of the most interesting materials for use in their stage plays: Plots to assassinate the queen, Jesuit subversions, secret alliances between English recusants and Roman Catholics abroad in favor of Mary Stuart's ascendancy, the St. Bartholomew's Day Massacre, the Invincible Spanish Armada, and other related enterprises are all reflected in various ways in the drama of the period. If the Settlement provided a point of view for dramatists, the religious controversy itself provided a mine of lively humor, intrigue, scenes of mystery and espionage, and quips at the common foe—none of which would have been lost on an Elizabethan audience.

While propaganda frequently appeared in support of the Elizabethan Settlement, and against a formidable national enemy, such elements tended to become less and less the main point of the dramatic works. Often they appeared only as a side issue or an occasional antipapal allusion. Of course, one must not forget that Elizabeth controlled stage plays through rather rigid censorship. A representative sampling of the dramatic fare that appeared after Elizabeth's accession is discussed in the following sections.

ACADEMIC DRAMA

The New Learning provided another phase in the development of drama through the introduction of imitations of Plautus and Terence in comedies and Seneca in tragedies. One of the most important developments in the history of Elizabethan drama was the introduction of the so-called Academic dramas which domesticated classical Roman examples and combined them with a thoroughly English spirit. With a sophisticated, intelligent audience, the possibilities for witty repartee and clever wordplay no doubt became more challenging for the successful dramatist. But whatever utilitarian and educational motives may have initiated such plays, by the middle of the sixteenth century they had outgrown any apparent motive other than that of pleasant entertainment.

One of the most celebrated of the Academic dramas is *Gammer Gurtons Nedle*, probably written by William Stevenson, a Cambridge scholar, for presentation at Christ's College. Of value in a discussion of the religious dispute is the treatment of the parish curate, Doctor Rat. Whether this delightful comedy was written during the last year of Edward's reign or during the early years of the Settlement would make minor difference in the curate's characterization because he is a stock figure of the Sir John type. His function in the drama is to provide rustic humor at the expense of an uncouth clergy—a stereotype retained from the medieval drama and still recognizable in the merry interludes of John Heywood.

Doctor Rat first becomes significant in *Gammer Gurtons Nedle*[1] in act 4 when he comes onstage and reveals an appreciable disparity between his real role as priest and the spiritual ideal to which he is committed. For example, he complains of having to be so busy in the interests of "such a sort" of parishioners that he is without "one pissing-while a day" to call his own. And worst of all, he must be "at euery knaues commaundement!" Not only does the curate resent his role as a minister, dedicated to the service of his flock, but he regrets that such a busy schedule prevents him from haunting the ale house as often as he would like.

> I had not sit the space to drinke two pots of ale
> But Gammer Gurtons sory boy was straiteway at my taile,
> And she was sicke, and I must come—to do I wot not what!   (4.1.6-8)

A Reformation or Settlement audience would have appreciated Doctor Rat's exposé of himself at this point, for Henry's First Royal Injunctions (1536) had stated positively that ecclesiastics were not to haunt taverns, but rather they were to spend their leisure time in study of the Scriptures or some useful exercise whereby they might set a good example for their parishioners at all times. This provision was repeated by Edward VI (1547) and Elizabeth (1559): ecclesiastics were forbidden to

---

[1]References are to the text in Joseph Quincy Adams, ed., *Chief Pre-Shakespearean Dramas* (Boston: Houghton Mifflin, 1924) 469-99.

resort to any taverns or ale houses, or to spend their time in "drinking or riot," or in playing at dice and cards. The fact that such an injunction was necessary at all indicates that some ecclesiastics were guilty of this offence.

On the other hand, since in all cases such injunctions came immediately following Reformation affirmations, the implication is that tavern and ale house "haunting" was characteristic of the Roman Catholic clergy, but not of Anglican ecclesiastics of the New Faith. If so, Doctor Rat's confession could easily be a mild jibe at a priest of the Old Faith. In either case, the humor derives from the discrepancy between the ideal and the real—the priest as he should be and as he actually is. In this function he differs little from Heywood's clerics, or even Chaucer's.

The playwright continues to expose the shortcomings of his priest when Doctor Rat complains of having to make what he considers unnecessary pastoral calls: "If once her [Gurton's] fingers-end but ake, 'Trudge!' Call for Doctor Rat!" (4.1.9). And the curate further reveals his spiritual failures when he implies that his pastoral duties are motivated by personal profit rather than by a sense of dedication to his mission in life.

> And when I come not at their call, I only thereby loose;
> For I am sure to lacke therefore a tythe-pyg or a goose.
> I warrant you, when truth is knowen, and told they haue their tale,
> The matter where-about I come is not worth a half-peny-worth of ale!
> Yet must I talke so sage and smothe as though I were glosier,
> Els, or the yere come at an end, I shal be sure the loser.   (4.1.11-16)

A Settlement audience's reaction to Doctor Rat's testimonial would have been that he deserves whatever abuse may come to him—perhaps as a matter of poetic justice. If this is the case, we are prepared for the curate's rough handling in scene 4, and the humor of his situation is easily justified. The fact that Elizabeth felt the necessity to order her subjects to respect ecclesiastics for what they represented indicates that there was no particular reverence among laymen for the priest as a man. It was then more a matter of reverence is as reverence does. Yet, despite Elizabeth's Injunctions, laying violent hands upon priests continued to be a subject of concern among clerics throughout the century. Consequently, Doctor Rat's well-deserved beating would no doubt have delighted the audience.

Doctor Rat violates ecclesiastical decorum, moreover, when he removes his clerical gown to become Diccon's dupe by crawling stealthily into a hole in Dame Chat's house, for a priest was at liberty to remove his habit only in the privacy of his home. The fact that he foolishly accepts Diccon's advice to enter Dame Chat's house secretly shows him to be indecorously meddlesome. The humor is thus heightened considerably when Dame Chat and her maids fall to beating the unwelcome intruder. Diccon, the comical Vice, suggests still more impropriety when he hears the fracas from his safe place outside the house, "Ware that! Hoow, my wenches! haue ye caught the foxe / That vsed to make reuel among your hennes and cocks?" (4.4.41-42). Moreover, Doctor Rat seems to forget the New Testament injunctions against personal vengeance and toward forgiveness of one's enemies when he pledges to get even with those who have thus used him.

> I will spend all I haue, without my skinne,
> But he shall be brought to the plight I am in!
> Master Bayly, I trow, and he be worth his eares,
> Will snaffle these murderers and all that them beares.
> I will surely neither byte nor suppe
> Till I fetch him hether, this matter to take vp.   (4.4.51-56)

Once it becomes apparent that Diccon has made a fool of him, the parish priest degrades his pastoral role by resorting to name calling of the most common sort: "He is the cause of all this brawle, that dyrty, shitten loute!" (5.2.183). Whether or not Diccon's aspersions against the curate are valid, he does imply that Doctor Rat's frequent visits to the tavern are responsible for the bruises on his head: "The horsen priest hath lift the pot in some of these alewyues chayres, / That his head wolde not serue him, belyke, to come down the stayres" (5.2.216-217).

Doctor Rat, still crying for vengeance, demands that Bayly take Diccon to the gallows. Yet even Bayly declares that such a demand ill befits an ecclesiastic.

> That ware to sore. A spiritual man to be so extreame!
> ....
> I graunt him wort[h]ie punishment, but in no wise so great.
>   (5.2.242,244)

Not only does the priest's ambiguous ethic come through in these allusions, but at the denouement Mayster Bayly indicates something of the ecclesiastic's reputation when he orders Diccon to compensate for Doctor Rat's injuries with sufficient ale, "And when ye meete at one pot, he shall haue the first pull, / And thou shalt neuer offer him the cup but it be full . . . " (5.2.276-277). Bayly's last words are to the effect that Doctor Rat should accept Gammer's invitation to visit the ale house to drink, for in that place the priest can appropriately warm and dress himself.

What we have in *Gammer Gurtons Nedle*, then, is a rustic curate used by the playwright for ribald, coarse humor. He is a fool, easily duped, and totally without the respect of his parishioners. Moreover, his own self-revelation shows he is unworthy as a cleric—hypocritical, worldly, vain, and given to vengeance. But what is important is the fact that the humor, though at the cleric's expense, is in good sport.

The priest's behavior would probably place him among pre-Reformation clerics of the Old Faith, yet his function in the play is not necessarily a malicious satire of corruption among the spiritualty as was ordinarily the case in Reformation polemical drama. Instead, Doctor Rat is a stock character retained from medieval literary convention. References to Reformation and Settlement restrictions upon clerical conduct would have provided the audience with a rationale for Doctor Rat's indelicate treatment on the stage without offending the truly pious.

Not so mild is the "mery" *Misogonus* (c. 1560-1577)[2] by an unknown dramatist. Prologus announces a brief resume of the play.

Whilum there in Laurentum dwelte—a towne of antike fame
in Italye, a countrey earst renounde with troiane knightes—
a gentleman whome Lott assinde Philogonus to name:
of this mannes destinies this tyme our author onely writes.
In lusty youth a wife he tooke, a dame of florishinge grene,
who sone after conceaude and brought him forth at once tootwinnes.
theldest she sente away, wherof hir husbande did not wene.
forthwith she died. at thother sonne our commody begins.
Through wanton educatione he begann to be contempteous
and sticked not with tauntinge tearmes his father to miscall
and straightway in lacivious luste he waxed so licentious,
thats father he did often vex and brought him to great thrall.
But lucklye lot yet at the lenghe his eldest sonne he knewe
and, yt he might his comforte be, sente for him in great hast.

---

[2]References are to the text in Alois Brandl, *Quellen des Weltlichen Dramas in England vor Shakespeare* (Strassburg: Karl J. Trübner, 1898) 409-89.

then after this the yonger sonne his life doth leade anewe,
wherat together all the ioy and bankett at the last.   (21-36)

It is a comedy of crude realism in which the prodigal son motif is
skillfully blended with the Italian comedy of lost children. Although the
play follows classical structure and cites Italy as its locale, it is thoroughly English in spirit.

The Protestant bias becomes apparent in act 2 when Misogonus,
sporting with the *morio* Cacurgus, offers to make the jester his personal
chaplain if he will reveal certain information for the prodigal's
advantage.

Yf it be for my wealth and for my advauntage,
Thou shalt be my chaplinge, I sweare by St. Loy;
Or if thou canst be prested, Ile giue the a persnage.   (1.3.42-44)

Aside from alluding to the general controversy concerning lay patronage
for ecclesiastics, the scene provides a little comic irreverence toward the
Roman Catholic clergy when Cacurgus takes up his master's proposal.

I thanke you; by my hallidome, I wer fit for that office,
I coulde mumble my mattinges and my durge with the best;
And if it were not for ye impostin in my kodpesse,
To lift at a chery I haue a buminge breaste.   (1.3.45-48)

This jab is only a mild satire of outmoded religious practices, and since
the words are spoken by the fool, they are more amusing than
controversial.

A more discernible animus comes through in act 2. In good Aristo-
telian tradition, a merry song enlivens the action of this Academic
drama. Cacurgus leads the others in singing a delightful song reminiscent of the goliardic drinking songs. One verse in particular identifies
the point of view.

We will therefore, for evermore,
               while this our life is lastinge,
[Eat], drinke and sleape and lemans kepe;
          [It's] poperye to vse fastinge.   (2.2.97-100)

The song, with its sweet rebellion against religious restrictions and social conformity, would no doubt have appealed to a college audience of
the Settlement period.

A more lively thrust at the clergy appears in scene 4 when Melissa the *meretrix* asks Misogonus to bring a companion into their revelries at the ale house to "make vs some sport." Immediately someone suggests Sir John the priest, for "neither cardes nor dice, I am sure, he doth lacke." Sir John's reputation in the ale house is apparently well known, because Orgelus (a servant of Misogonus) implies that the cleric is no different from the rest of their company: "How doth he differ, I pray yow, from the reste? / He is no more a prist than yow ar, and he were out of his gowne" (2.4.47-48).

Oenophilus, another servant, defends the priest with a dubious encomium.

> Disdayne yow? Sir John as good as yow will haue his companye,
> As the fellowlist prist that is in this shire;
> To all the lusty guttes he is knowne for his honestye;
> Has not one dropp of pristes bloud in him, my thinke I durst swere.
>
> (2.4.49-52)
> ....
> Both at cardes and dice I knowe him to be skillful;
> Heile not stick to daunce, if company befalle him;
> In game with a gentleman heile never be wilfull.   (2.4.58-60)

Orgelus adds to Sir John's public reputation by saying that the priest "is not with out a dosin pare of dice," and he is probably now playing cards or else at some other game table. Sir John is not like the Reformed clerics, "this new start vp rables," for

> Thers no honest pastime but he putes it in sure,
> Not one game comes vpp but he has it bith backe,
> Everye wench ith townes acquainted with his lure;
> Its pittye (so god helpe me) that ever he shoulde lacke.   (2.4.64-67)
> ....
> Theirs to fewe such as he is, he would make you a fine mann.
> Heile not bash to grope a trul to smacke and to kisse.
> We haue daunct and carded a hole weke and nere blanne.   (2.4.98-100)

When Sir John comes onstage, he quickly confirms whatever rumors have circulated about his reputation.

> If your worshipp lack a gamster and a gamster very fayre,
> For a pound or two Ile kepe yow company by day or by night.
> At cardes, dice or tables or anythinge I will not spare;
> To kepe a gentleman compa[ny] I doe greatly delighte.   (2.4.113-116)

To the *meretrix*, Sir John says that he can play at many games, such as "ruff, mawe, and saint"; moreover, "Dice I haue plenty, yow shall see them in hast; / Heirs even my study, if I hit of good licker" (2.4.131-132).

The humor of the situation is increased considerably when Sir John wagers his clerical gown against Cacurgus's gown in a game of cards, and more humorous yet, the priest loses: "Done, Sir John, twenty pound, I haue wonn the priestes gowne; / Looke here, my masters, doe yow not knowe him bi his shankes?" (2.4.141-142). One can imagine the comic effect of Sir John's having to expose his bare legs to the audience.

When the group switches to throwing dice, Sir John continues to add humor to the already amusing spectacle by uttering oaths before and after casting: "By the motherkine a god," "a pox consume it," "by god and all the world," "by ye body of our lorde Jesus Christe." Sir John becomes so much absorbed in his game that he refuses to stop long enough to answer the call of the church bells for vespers: "He play still, come out what will, He never giue over ith lurtch; / Let them ringe till their arses ake, I knowe the worste" (2.4.209-210).

Despite Orgelus's attempt to shame the priest into returning to his church where the congregation awaits his service, Misogonus tells him to continue his game, and he offers to intercede on his behalf should he be called before the ordinary. Sir John answers, "By god, I thanke you, Sir; my parishioners, I am sure, be content / To misse service one night, so they knowe I am well occupied" (2.4.217-218). Sir John then wagers his entire benefice on a throw of the dice. But just then, his clerk Jacke arrives to summon the priest to the church.

The satire shifts to a *reductio ad absurdum* of the Roman Catholic service when Sir John directs his clerk to say the service during the priest's absence. Since it is not the Lenten season, it does not matter. "Fayth, Jacke, its no matter, an all thy lessons be lackinge; / Say a magnificat nunc dimittis, an even end with the crede" (2.4.239-240). Orgelus perceptively asks, "What, shall he leaue out ye saumes and his pater noster? / What good will ye crede doe without thos and his avy?" (2.4.241-242).

Clerk Jacke tells Sir John that if he knew who was present in the church he would leave his dice at once. To this the depraved priest responds just as the audience may have expected: "Is susan swetlips come? mas, Jacke, Ile go sear; / Pray you, Sir, giue me leaue but even go to tourne him my booke" (2.4.247-248). But at Melissa's entreaty, Sir John decides to remain for more sport while Jacke attends to the service.

When the *meretrix* invites Sir John to dance with her, he replies characteristically, "By S. patrike, damsell, for your sake Ile out vaunce; / Its good to fetch a friske once a day, I fynde it in my texte" (2.4.263-264). Once they begin dancing, Melissa tells the priest that he is the best dancer of any priest she has ever known. Orgelus, becoming jealous, says of their dancing, "Bith marye god, howe lustelye the lubber nowe skipps! / Gods precious, the skabb with my mistrisse doth tupe" (2.4.283-284). The others laugh at Cacurgus's jealousy, but he, seeking revenge, rushes out of the tavern just as Philogonus, Misogonus's father, and Eupelas, Philogonus's neighbor, enter.

The scene thus far has been highly amusing. It contains all the elements of comedy which have delighted audiences through the years, but now the Vices have become more mischievous than malicious, and their rascality is in good sport. But Sir John, while differing little from the medieval Sir John literary type, seems to represent the depraved and corrupt stereotype of the Roman Catholic cleric.

Sir John in the tavern would easily bring to mind the royal injunctions against priests who haunt taverns, play at cards, dice, and other game tables, and are negligent in their offices. To a Settlement audience, the coarse self-revelation of Sir John would probably confirm the government's propaganda, both from tractates and pulpit, that stated that Romanist or "popish" priests were corrupt and avaricious. Of course, these derogatory allusions to the Roman Catholic service also help sustain the satire.

Yet, the tavern scene is good comedy, and skillfully handled—even to the inclusion of spectacle and dance—so that the possible polemics do not come through. What we have, even for the audience of scholars, is vulgar comedy in high style. The satire is effective, the action is lively, and the characters in the tavern are all Vice characters, but the total effect is not malicious. It is merely delightful in spite of latent animosity toward the Old Faith.

When Philogonus comes onstage the mirth continues, but Sir John is given more opportunity to reveal some of the practices Elizabeth found objectionable among clerics of the older form. For example, Sir John attempts to defend the coarse companions of the noble's son by implying that he has married Misogonus to Melissa: "What, if this gentlewoman and your sonne I have maried, / May they not then come together without any offence?" (2.5.25-26). Philogonus answers with repugnance, "Ide rather thou wert hanged theife and he to his graue caried / Thon to marye him (varlat) without my licens" (2.5.27-28).

Elizabeth had decreed that her ecclesiastics could not perform marriages without parental consent. Moreover, without parental consent such marriages were invalid. By implication, this was not always the case among Roman Catholic clerics. One recalls, for example, the marriage between Romeo and Juliet performed without parental knowledge or consent by Friar Laurence. Nevertheless, the general lack of respect for clerical persons among the laity can be imagined in light of the words of neighbor Eupelas to the priest.

> Hast thou maried him, priest, then vnknitt me this knott.
> Darst thou kepe company with another mans wife?
> Thou abhominable sodomit, thou execrable sott,
> So god shall iudge me, pild Jacke, its pittye of thy life.   (2.5.29-32)

Eupelas becomes the stern voice of the Settlement when he rebukes Sir John. Not only does he allude to the priest's spiritual negligence, but he also provides a thrust at the "idolotrous" forms of the Romanist liturgy.

> Dost thou but what thou shouldst doe, yn Idolatrouse heste;
> Shouldst thou be the ringleader in dauncinge this while?
> A good minister would be at church now, attendinge one gods heaste.
> Of all wreches that ever I knewe thou are most vile.   (2.5.37-40)

Liturgus (Philogonus's servant) repeats a common proverb to prove the meddlesomeness of priests: "Thers no mischeife, as they say commenly, but a priest at one end . . . " (2.5.73).

Sir John, now completely out of character as a man of God, suggests personal vengeance upon the one speaking the proverb, and he shows his general disregard for respectable company: "When soever I mete yow, sir, looke your head that yow find! / A fart for yow all; come, Melissa, ile away" (2.5.76-77). In good Reformation spirit, Eupelas consoles the despairing Philogonus after Misogonus defies him openly: "The best is for yow to trust in Christ Jhesus alone / And by faith in his mercy your self for to stay" (2.5.103-104).

The comical mood has been quickly dispelled. The mirth and gay rebellion of the tavern has been superseded by an inevitable sympathy with the sufferings of the father for his prodigal son. The second act closes with old Philogonus pouring out his grief in a "dolefull dittye" to the

Lord. He blames only himself for not providing proper discipline for the formative years of his son's life, and he prays, "Pardon for that is past I craue / With hope some helpe of the to haue" (2.5.175-176).

Another intrusion of Settlement theology occurs in act 3 in a scene between the rustic tenant Codrus and his master Philogonus. The poor ignorant man is about to reveal to Philogonus the fact that Misogonus has a twin brother yet living, although it has been a carefully guarded secret since the child's infancy. Apparently only the rustic and his wife know about it. But first Codrus refers to the dead wife of Philogonus and says that he offers a prayer for her soul every night according to the Old Faith, " . . . thers near a day but I haue hir in my bede role; / I say a de profundus for hir erie night according toth olde rate" (3.1.151-152).

Philogonus corrects this Roman Catholic practice of praying for the dead, and he recites the teaching of the New Faith.

> Pray for hir no more, but rather giue god praise;
> Your praires are but superstitions and she, I hopes, at rest.
> Yow loue hir, it semes; so did I, and shall doe all my daies.
> But now to praye for our selves here, while we liue,
>   I count it best.   (3.1.153-156)

Codrus recognizes Philogonus as a man of the New Faith: "Low yow, Alison, were Moster is oth new larninge; did not I tell yow before?" (3.1.157).

Prayers for the dead had been among the first of the Romanist practices abolished by the zealous Reformers under Edward VI. While legislation regarding chantries had begun during the reign of Henry VIII (1545), it was not until the appearance of Edward's Act Dissolving the Chantries (1547) that attention was focused upon the theological assumptions that permitted prayers for the dead. Edward's act referred to prayers for the dead and requiem masses as "superstition and errors" induced by ignorance. By the time of the Settlement, prayers for the dead had become generally associated with the Old Faith.

The dramatist makes another thrust at the papacy, and by extension at the general "superstition" of the Roman Catholic practices, when the Vice Cacurgus (disguised as a magician) tells his audience about a cure for their ills. The cure results from a combination of "an herbe cald envy," "hipocrase that growes in ery garden," "tow drames of lecherye," "Infidelitye," and "an ownce of poperye." The allusion may be somewhat subtle when compared to other anti-Romanist derogation, but here it also serves as effective drama as well as polemics. That is, Cacurgus in this scene is a retention of the medieval Vice in disguise that had long been popular on the stage. The retention of the medieval device of allegory now becomes palatable when it merely names the Vices mentioned in the cure rather than attempting to personify them as living figures onstage. At the same time, polemics is served by the fact that the references are spoken by the Vice himself—a charlatan. By associating "poperye" with envy, infidelity, lechery, and hypocrisy, the dramatist assures that the audience could not fail to get the meaning. The audience would also have known that Cacurgus's pretended powers to cure ills and to read palms were in violation of Elizabeth's Royal Injunctions.

The same type of mild derogation of Roman Catholic services appears briefly in act 4. The rustic Codrus recalls having been taught the "patnuster" of the Old Faith, and he says, "I ha sounge yet: cum spiritu tuo with preist ith kirke, when wer howlinge" (4.1.142). Allusions to the Roman Catholic insistence upon saying the service in Latin rather than in the vernacular continued to appear in the Settlement drama.

Misogonus is significant as a work in which the materials of the ecclesiastical controversy are handled so skillfully that they do not depreciate conscious art. Sir John in the tavern among the revellers is effective comedy, and he is little more than his medieval progenitors. Thus his depiction as a lecherous, avaricious, worldly, meddlesome, and indolent ecclesiastic of the Old Faith provides good comedy.

However, the attention of this play is focused away from the priest, and, unlike most of the earlier Sir John plays, it is focused upon doctrinal points of the ecclesiastical controversy. That is, instead of merely providing a humorous depiction of a corrupt cleric, the dramatist also uses association to ridicule some of the doctrinal beliefs of the Old Faith, such as the confessional, prayers for the dead, intercession of saints, images, and lay patronage.

Also significant is the dramatist's ability to handle controversial material in the play so skillfully that it does not detract from the lively humor. Assuming the Anglican bias of an educated Settlement audience committed to the New Learning, we can see that Roman Catholic doctrinal and devotional differences seem to be associated with ignorance, medievalism, and religious practices currently out of vogue. It is good drama, not because it includes controversial and relevant material of its age, but because it uses this contemporary material the way it should always be used in art—as subordinate to the main theme.

There are other examples of the religious controversy in other Academic plays, such as *The Disobedient Child, All for Money*, and *The Contract of Marriage between Wit and Wisdom*. These plays demonstrate the manner in which materials of the ecclesiastical controversy were used for humor and lively action onstage. Generally speaking, the Academic drama shares a kinship with the interludes of John Heywood in method;[3] yet, themes other than the corruption of clerics are used effectively, as *Misogonus* demonstrates. Academic drama tends to move the central interest away from the cleric and make of him a side issue. Related items of the religious dispute become little more than contemporary subjects, often mentioned or portrayed only in passing.

ELIZABETHAN INTERLUDES

Although Queen Elizabeth's restrictions upon the drama would appear to have prohibited the popular stage from either improperly treating matters of religion or from entering into religious controversy,[4] certain of the interludes continued to employ such materials effectively to reinforce the doctrinal position of the Settlement or to attack the seeming idolatry, superstition, and tyranny of the Old Faith.

One of the most representative plays of this genre is Nathaniel Wood's *Conflict of Conscience* (c. 1570). It was based upon a famous contemporary event—the "apostasy" and consequent despair of "Frauncis Spera" (Francesco Spiera), an Italian lawyer who defected from Protestantism.[5]

Conflict of Conscience, like some of the other interludes, contains many of the conventions of the Morality play, which apparently continued to have popular appeal even while other genres were developing collaterally. For example, most of the characters are allegorical, although

---

[3]For an example of John Heywood's use of ecclesiastical materials in one interlude, see my article, "*The Pardoner and the Friar* as Reformation Polemic," in *Renaissance Papers 1971* (Duke University, Durham NC: Southeastern Renaissance Conference, 1972) 17-24.

[4]See "Injunctions of Elizabeth," articles 50 and 51, in Gee and Hardy, 417-42.

[5]For an account of Spiera and other possible sources for the play, see Celesta Wine, "Nathaniel Wood's *Conflict of Conscience*," *PMLA* 50 (September 1935): 661-78.

some are intended to be personal. The stage directions suggest that the *dramatis personae* can be "deuided into six partes, most conuenient for such as be disposed, either to shew this Comedie in priuate houses, or otherwise."[6]

The interlude is divided into six acts, the last of which is no more than an epilogue spoken by the Nuntius. Yet the whole is designed to teach a moral lesson to the audience—"stir up their minds to godliness, which should it see or hear . . . " (p. 32).

The Prologue briefly declares the argument of the play.

> The argument or ground, whereon our Author chiefly stayed,
> Is (sure) a history strange and true, to many men well known,
> Of one through love of worldly wealth and fear of death dismay'd,
> Because he would his life and goods have kept still as his own,
> From state of grace wherein he stood was almost overthrown;
> So that he had no power at all in heart firm faith to have,
> Till at the last God chang'd his mind his mercies for to crave.   (p. 32)

Yet, explains the Prologue, since the story is "too-too dolorous" and would constrain one "with tears of blood his cheeks to wet," the author has intermixed "some honest mirth," though being careful to observe decorum.

The decorum, however, is purely aesthetic. Immediately after these words, the arch-Vice enters to explain his purpose in the world: He is Satan himself. In a long oration he explains that since the kingdom of this world has been allotted to him, he in turn has bestowed it upon the pope, "my darling dear, whose faithful love I know, / Shall never fail from me, but daily flow," since the pope best imitates the devil's dealings and "doth pursue God's laws with deadly hate." Satan says the pope is his own son who elevates himself above all humanity.

> So that in *terris Deus sum*, saith he:
> In earth I am a God, with sins for to dispense,
> And for rewards I will forgive each manner of offence.   (p. 36)

The dramatist then attempts to parallel the work of the papacy with Satan's own temptations, and in doing so he repeats the conventional aspersions of the Roman Catholic system. Satan continues his oration,

---

[6]References are to the text in Robert A. Dodsley, *A Select Collection of Old English Plays*, 4th ed. (London: Reeves and Turner, 1874-1876) 6:31-142.

I said to Eve: tush, tush, thou shalt not die,
But rather shalt as God know everything;
My son likewise, to maintain idolatry,
Saith: tush, what hurt can carved idols bring?
Despise this law of God, the heavenly King,
And set them in the church for men thereon to look:
An idol doth much good: it is a layman's book.   (p. 36)

The Reformation belief that images were idolatrous in the churches was persistent. The last words quoted above seem to exceed Henry's Second Royal Injunctions (1538) which had permitted the use of images insofar as they were not themselves objects of worship: they "serve for no other purpose but as to be books of unlearned men that cannot know letters . . . "[7] But Elizabeth's Injunctions (1559) had ordered ecclesiastics to destroy images.[8] Wood's allusion to images' being idolatrous seems to reinforce Elizabeth's Settlment program regulating all objects of superstition.

Satan enumerates other "pretty toys" that the pope ("my boy") has devised to keep human souls from hell, regardless how "wickedly" they may live on earth. Some of these "toys" are "masses, trentals, pardons, and scala coeli." All these practices of the Old Faith had been abolished by the Elizabethan Settlement. Moreover, Wood draws another parallel between Satan and the pope by referring to the religious martyrs during the Marian Persecution.

I egged on Pharoah, of Egypt the king,
The Israelites to kill, so soon as they were born:
My darling likewise doth the selfsame thing,
And therefore causes kings and princes to be sworn,
That with might and main they shall keep up his horn,
And shall destroy with fire, axe, and sword,
Such as against him shall speak but one word.   (p. 37)

The Smithfield fires were still fresh in the minds of many who may have seen the play, but such a charge against the papacy was too common during Elizabeth's reign to require a specific reference.

---

[7]See "Second Royal Injunctions," article 7, in Gee and Hardy, 275-81.

[8]See "Injunctions of Elizabeth," article 23, in Gee and Hardy, 417-22.

Satan announces that he has provided the pope with two champions to fight in his behalf: Avarice and Tyrannical Practice.

> For, as I said, although I claim by right
> The kingdom of this earthly world so round,
> And in my stead to rule with force and might
> I have assigned the Pope, whose match I nowhere found,
> His heart with love to me so much abound . . .   (p. 38)

To help the champions lure men into their train, Satan will send Hypocrisy into the world. Before making his exit, Satan promises to send forth these imps from hell to assume their human forms.

There is little action in the opening scene, but the effect of bringing Satan onstage in whatever elaborate costume he wore was no doubt exciting. As Satan praises his son, the pope becomes Satan's vicar by association and, therefore, a principal Vice in disguise. The technique is not new, but it is more skillfully handled by Wood than by most before him. Such a depiction of the pope is necessary for the point of view, for all the sufferings which are to follow in the play are the result of the pope's grand design to usurp God's prerogatives with the aid of Avarice, Tyrannical Practice, and Hypocrisy.

Yet, while the dramatic technique is aided thereby, the cause of antipapal propaganda is served simultaneously. One needs only to recall Jewel's *Apology*, the *Book of Homilies* (1562), and certain of the propaganda tracts of the period to realize how closely Wood's references to the pope follow them.

In scene 2 Philologus and Mathetes discuss the "misery" of their days which must be sustained by "Romish hypocrisy." Philologus, in good Protestant tradition, recounts the various martyrdoms of the Apostles and Old Testament figures, and he concludes that it is better to suffer death for the sake of truth than to live in error. Getting to the point of the discussion, he says, "The Pope at this instant sundry torments procure, / For such as by God's holy word will endure" (p. 41).

From the Scriptures Philologus determines to learn two things:

> The first is God's church from the devil's to discern:
> The second to mark what manifest resistance
> The truth of God hath, and what encumbrance
> It bringeth upon them that will it profess;
> Wherefore they must arm themselves to suffer distress.   (p. 42)

Therefore, persecution of Christ's Church can be beneficial in that it fortifies the faithful and teaches them to call upon God in times of affliction. Paraphrasing the book of Romans he says, "For trouble brings forth patience, from patience doth ensue / Experience, from experience hope, of health the anchor true" (p. 43).

The purpose of this scene is to explain the nature of adversity among the faithful and to prepare the audience for what is to come later when Philologus chooses to relieve his own affliction by unworthy motives. Frequent references to Scripture in the scene bring to mind the Reformation emphasis upon the vernacular Bible in the hands of laymen. But the use of Scripture here demonstrates how closely allied the drama was with the sermon. Not only does Philologus know the contents of biblical passages, he can recite chapter references, just as the author had done in antipapal sermons from his pulpit in Norwich. For example, "Which thing our Saviour Christ doth teach, as testifieth Luke, / The thirteenth chapter, where he doth vainglorious men rebuke" (p. 44).

On the other hand, the Council of Trent in 1546 had decreed that the traditions of Church Fathers were equal in value and authority to the Scriptures: God is the author of the Scriptures, and church tradition was "dictated by Christ or by the Holy Spirit."[9] Both, according to Roman Catholic orthodoxy, are equally inspired and of equal value and dignity. The Settlement consistently maintained that the Scriptures were the sole authority in matters of faith, while Church tradition was created by the authority of humanity.

In the second scene of act 2, Tyranny and Avarice explain the nature of their work. Tyranny says that he will "charm" the tongues of those who oppose his will with "fire and sword" and other torments. He also complains about the increasing numbers of the faithful who have sprung

---

[9]Council of Trent, session 4, April 1546. See Bettenson, 367. John Foxe recorded a dispute between Alexander Alefius and Bishop Stokeley of London in Convocation (c. 1540). Stokeley defended the Romanist position: "Finally wee haue receiued many things of the doctors and councels by times, which forsomuch as the old doctors of the Church doe make mention of them, we ought to grant that we receiued them of the Apostles, and that they be of like authority with the scripture, and finally that they may worthily be called the word of God unwritten." *Acts and Monvments of Matters Most Speciall and Memorable, Happening in the Church with an Historie of the Same* (London: 1631-1632) 2:506. Foxe's work is generally referred to by its more commonly known title, Foxe's *Book of Martyrs*.

up *because* he has refrained from killing heretics. But all this will change, for he promises to shed enough blood in the future to prevent their increase.

> For if I hear of any that in word or in deed—
> Yea, if it be possible to know their intent,
> If I can prove that in thought they it meant
> To impair our estates—no prayer shall serve,
> But will pay them their hire, as each one deserve.   (p. 49)

Meanwhile, as the Vices are boasting of their future triumphs, Hypocrisy provides some satiric humor by making side remarks. For example, after the boast of Tyranny quoted above, Hypocrisy says, "A popish policy!" and "Anti-christian charity." Avarice suggests that since they have had a free hand in the past, the faithful will probably be wary of them in the future, remembering the sufferings they have gone through.

The allusion here suggests a campaign to restore Roman Catholic jurisdiction in England, such as was the case during Mary Tudor's reign. If so, the whole scene would have greater relevance to the contemporary audience during the first decade of the Settlement. Parliament expressed this fear as early as 1563 when it enacted legislation motivated by the potential danger of "the enemy as well here bred amongst us as abroad." Englishmen feared that the pope would attempt to regain England for the Roman See by ordering an invasion by loyal Roman Catholic countries on the Continent. This fear continued until the end of Elizabeth's reign.

Tyranny suggests that Avarice's fear of failure to impose the pope's will upon the people is unwarranted since the Reformed clergy will recant out of personal gain.

> In the clergy, I know, no friends we shall want,
> Which for hope of gain the trust will recant,
> And give themselves wholly to set out Hypocrisy,
> Being egg'd on with Avarice, and defended by Tyranny.   (p. 50)

Avarice agrees that the clergy will help them, because they gained the most profit before the Settlement, but the laity present a different matter.

> Well may the clergy on our side hold,
> For they by us no small gain did reap;
> But all the temporalty, I dare be bold

To venture in wager of gold a good heap,
At our preferments will mourn, wail, and weep.   (p. 50)

But, says Tyranny, the laity will alter their minds out of fear of the
sword.

The entire scene is a masterful piece of antipapal propaganda, for it
exploits the natural fears of Englishmen during the period. With subtle
reminders of what the nation had suffered under Queen Mary, the Settlement audience could more easily associate the boasts and threats of
the Vices with something that had happened in the recent past and
which could happen again.

Hypocrisy joins Avarice and Tyranny, and after a tedious altercation,
he announces his part in the plan.

. . . the Pope and I together have devised,
Firstly to inveigle the people religious,
For greediness of gain who will be soon pressed:
And, for fear lest hereafter they should be despised,
Of their own freewill will maintain Hypocrisy,
So that Avarice alone shall conquer the clergy.
Now, of the chiefest of his carnal cardinals
He doth appoint certain, and give them authority
To ride abroad in their pontificals,
To see if with Avarice they may win the laity;
If not, then to threaten them with open Tyranny:
Whereby doubt not but many will forsake
The truth of the gospel, and our parties take.   (p. 50)

The insertion of this program to put down the Reformation is important
for the crisis of the play. That is, Wood's underlying thesis thus far has
been that the faithful Christian must endure persecution for the gospel's
sake, regardless of the promise of rewards for yielding to the pope's
tyranny.

Persecution will come, but it, like all adversity, must be accepted as
a part of God's will through which His mercy can be made manifest. Hypocrisy maintains that the clergy will be the first to yield to the pope, for
they have the most to gain; yet, they will hide behind Hypocrisy to avoid
being despised for their defection. Like the clergy, many of the laity will
yield under the threat of punishment. The protagonist will have to make
his decision to renounce the Reformation against his own knowledge of
the truth and the theology of suffering.

In act 3, Philologus announces in a set speech that the papal legate from Rome has arrived in the realm.

Who doth the saints of God each where with tyranny oppress,
And in the same most gloriously himself he vaunt and boast:
The more one mourneth unto him he pitieth the less.   (p. 64)

Philologus considers his many worldly holdings, his family, and his friends and decides that if he wants to keep them he must renounce his faith: "Which if I do, without all doubt my soul for aye I spill" (p. 64). But because he cannot find a way out of his personal dilemma, he continues in indecision.

Scene 3 contains the assumption that the restoration of papal jurisdiction is already well underway. Avarice instructs Tyranny how to proceed with his design.

I would have you show rigour to such as resist,
And such as be obstinate spare not to kill;
But those that be willing your hests to fulfil,
If they offend, and not of obstinacy,
For money excuse them, though they use villany,
Thus shall you perform your office aright,
For favour or money to spare the offendent.   (pp. 67-68)

Lest the audience fail to recognize the intended thrust, Wood causes Hypocrisy to say aside, "Hark the practice of spiteful Sumnors." Avarice then tells the other Vices the contents of the papal legate's commission which is to be effected immediately.

He hath firstly in charge to make inquisition,
Whether altars be re-edified, whether chalice and book,
Vestments for mass, sacraments, and procession,
Be prepared again: if not, he must look,
And find out such fellows as these cannot brook,
And to my Lord Legate such merchants present,
That for their offence they may have condign punishment.   (pp. 69-70)

Wood seems to have in mind the Injunctions of Elizabeth (1559), which had ordered, among denunciations of other practices quoted above, that altars should be removed from churches and in their place a communion table was to be provided.[10] The other items mentioned had been abolished by the Settlement.

Caconos, a priest, comes onstage in scene 4, and speaking in a northern dialect, he announces that the pope once again has been restored to the land. He says that the papal legate goes throughout the country with authority,

> And charge befare him far te com us priests end lemen hath,
> Far te spay awt, gif that he mea, these new-sprang arataics,
> Whilk de disturb aur hally Kirk, laik a sart of saysmatics.   (pp. 70-71)

The village priest goes on to explain something of the successful restoration of the Old Faith in his own land.

> Awr gilden Gods ar brought ayen intea awr kirks ilkwhare,
> That unte tham awr parishioner ma offer thar gude-will.
> For hally mass in ilk place new thea autars de prepare,
> Hally water, pax, cross, banner, censer and candill,
> Cream, crismatory, hally bread, the rest omit ay will,
> Whilt hally fathers did invent fre awd antiquity,
> Be new received inte awr kirks with great solemnity.   (p. 71)

Yet, he says, clerics profit by the restoration of these practices, although the laymen ("lemen") are oppressed as a result. He recognizes that some of the Roman Catholic practices are fraudulent, intended to deceive the temporalty for economic profit.

> Awr hally mass, thaw thea bay dere, thea de it but in vain,
> Far thaw ther frends frea Purgatory te help thea dea believe,
> Yet af ther hope, gif need rewhayre, it wawd theam all deceive.
> Sea wawd awr pilgrimage, reliques, trentals, and pardons,
> Whilk far awr geyn inte awr Kirk ar braught in far the nonce.   (p. 71)
> . . . .
> Sawl-masses, diriges, monethmayndes and buryings,
> Alsowlnday, kirkings, banasking and weddings.
> The sacraments, gif we mowt sell, war better than thea all;
> Far gif the Jews gave thratty pence te hang Chraist on a tree,
> Gude Christian folk thrayse thratty pence wawd count a price but small;
> Sea that te eat him with their teeth delaivered he mawght be.
> New of this thing delaiverance ne man can make but we,

---

[10]See "Injunctions of Elizabeth," articles 23 and 24, in Gee and Hardy, 417-42.

Se that the market in this punt we priests sawd han at will,
And with the money we sowd yet awr pooches we sowd fill.   (p. 72)

The point of all this matter is that the papacy insists upon maintaining Old Faith practices out of personal gain. The clergy is willing to acquiesce, although they know that such practices are deceptive, because they also share in the profits derived from such restoration. The items enumerated here and the attitude expressed by Caconos represent the essence of pulpit and pamphlet propaganda during the Settlement period.

The scene proceeds with dubious warrant even as propaganda. It is too dull for entertainment, and it is too tedious for effective propaganda. There is no conscious humor to amuse the audience, a device used effectively in the Academic drama with much better results. Wood misses a great opportunity for lively action and witty self-revelation by Caconos with his "Scottish" dialect, but since he apparently lacks a sense of good dramatic technique, the preacher in Wood submerges the artist. He takes himself too seriously, and the drama suffers as a result.

When Wood attempts to employ humor in the scene it is generally in the satiric responses of the priest, although the humor of such responses may not have been intentionally humorous in all cases. For example, Tyranny, in the spirit of Elizabeth's ecclesiastical visitors, greets the priest and tells him, "I have a commission your house and church to seek, / To search if you any seditious books do keep" (p. 73). Caconus responds, "Whe ay? well a near, ay swear bay the Sacrament, / Ay had rather han a cup of nale than a Testament" (p. 73). Hypocrisy asks the priest how it is possible for him to discharge his office without a Testament, and Caconus responds to this question in a similiar fashion.

It is the least thing ay car far, bay may charge;
Far se lang as thea han images wharon te luke,
What need thea be distructed awt af a buik?   (p. 73)

Wood's satire is more effectively handled when he reveals Caconus as an ignorant priest of the Old Faith who cannot read the Latin of his breviary, but instead must guess at the holy days by looking at the illuminated letters.

As far example: on the day of Chraist's nativity,
Ay see a bab in a manger and two beasts standing by:
The service whilk to Newyear's-day is assign'd
Bay the paicture of the circumscision ay faynd:

The service, whilk on Twalfth-day mun be done,
Ay seeke bay the mark of the three kings of Cologne.   (pp. 73-74)

The priest explains that his parishioners pray to the various saints represented on the church walls.

Se the sandry mairacles, whilk ilk sent have done,
Bay the pictures on the walls sal appear to them soon,
Bay the whilk thea ar learned in every distress,
What sent thea mun prea te far succour, doubtless:
Sea that all lepers to Sylvester must prea,
That he wawd frae tham ther disease take away.   (p. 74)

A Settlement audience would have found the lengthy catalogue of patron saints designated to heal various diseases amusing, since Elizabeth's Injunctions had expressly forbidden such "superstitious" practices. Elizabeth had also ordered clerics to destroy "pictures, paintings, and all other monuments of feigned miracles," including stained glass windows and representations of miracles upon church walls.[11] On the other hand, in his *Spiritual Exercises* (1548) Loyola had instructed the Jesuits to venerate and invoke the saints, as had the Council of Trent (1563).[12] Elizabethans considered the invocation of saints superstitious and idolatrous, and they associated it with ignorance and papal innovation. It was contrary to the spirit of the New Learning and without scriptural authority.

When Tyranny asks Caconos if there are any "schismatics" in his parish, the priest replies that there is a "busybody" who makes sport of him, calls him "fule and noddy," and "sets his lads te spout Latin ayenst me." Moreover, he continues, the heretic argues with him about the doctrine of transubstantiation.

And oftentimes he will reason with me of the Sacrament,
And say he can prove bay the New Testament

---

[11]See "Injunctions of Elizabeth," article 23, in Gee and Hardy, 417-42.

[12]It is possible that Wood's long catalogue of special saints (pp. 74-75) was motivated by the recent decision of the Council of Trent (1563) to order the teaching of "intercession of saints, the invocation of saints, the honor due to relics, and the lawful use of images; teaching them [the people] that the Saints who reign with Christ offer their prayers to God on behalf of men, that it is good and useful to invoke them in supplication and to have recourse to their prayers, their help and their succor for the obtaining of benefits from God . . . " (session 25). Bettenson, 372-73.

That Chraist's body is in heaven placed;
But ays not believe him, ay woll not be awt-faced.　　(p. 76)

The doctrine of transubstantiation had been argued persistently throughout the early years of the Reformation. Henry VIII first made the doctrine a test of faith and regarded its rejection as punishable by death for treason and heresy, stating the penalty clearly in the Six Articles Act (1539). Protestants more zealous than Henry managed to reject the doctrine as impossible in the Forty-two Articles (1553) under Edward VI. Convocation altered Cranmer's Forty-two Articles to the present Thirty-nine Articles in 1563. Thus Caconos's "heretic" was a good Anglican.

Caconos continues to describe the "schismatic" in his parish by mentioning the man's abuse of the Roman pontiff.

He says besayd that the Pope is Antichraist,
Fugered of John bay the seven-headed beast,
And all awre religion is but mon's invention,
And with God's ward is at utter dissension;
And a plaguy deal ware of sayk layk talk,
That ay dar not far may narse bay his yate walk,
But aw wawd he wer brunt, that ay mawght be whaiet.　　(p. 76)

The "schismatic" sounds like the author of some antipapal passages in the *Book of Homilies* (1562), perhaps even Bishop Jewel, because in that book the Church of Rome is spoken of as being idolatrous, "being indeed not only a harlot (as the Scripture calleth her) but also a foul, filthy, old, withered, harlot (for she is indeed of ancient years) . . . the great strumpet of all strumpets, the mother of whoredom set forth by St. John in his Revelation."[13] Of course, abuse of the pope as the Antichrist is characteristic of Settlement pulpit and pamphlet propaganda. Jewel's *Apology* is replete with such abuses of the pope, as was stated earlier. This monumental work enumerates Roman Catholic practices that Jewel regarded as innovations by the papacy and unsupported by Scriptures.

Caconos names the "heretic" in his parish as Philologus ("Phailelegoos"). The Vices then exit as Hypocrisy attempts to provide a merry

---

[13]*Certaine Sermons or Homilies*, vol. 2, ch. 2, pt. 3, p. 69.

song for some much needed mirth. The scene as a whole seems to be an apology for the Settlement.

In act 4 all the Vices confront the protagonist. Cardinal, the papal legate, arrives on the scene and addresses Tyranny, now disguised appropriately as Zeal: "Go to, Master Zeal, bring forth that heretic, / Which doth thus disturb our religion catholic" (p. 78). Wood employs another popular device of the drama by setting up a trial of Philologus in a mock consistory court. Hypocrisy acts as the legate's "notary" to record the proceedings. Cardinal charges the prisoner.

> Ah, sirrah! be you he that doth thus disturb
> The whole estate of our faith catholic?
> Art thou so expert in God's laws and word,
> That no man may learn thee, thou arrant heretic?
> But this is the nature of every schismatic:
> Be his errors never so false doctrine,
> He will say by God's word he dare it examine.   (pp. 79-80)

Philologus tells Cardinal that he will answer every question according to conscience, "God's word being my warrant." The dramatist then strikes at the heart of the Roman Catholic position when he causes Cardinal to ask the essential question:

> Have I authority to call thee me before?
> Or, to be short, I will object it thus:
> Whether hath the Pope, which is Peter's successor,
> Than all other bishops preheminence more?
> If not, then it follow that neither he,
> Nor I which am his legate, to accompts may call thee.   (p. 80)

The whole authority of the pontiff rests upon the answer. One recalls that immediately following Henry's excommunication (1553) he challenged his bishops to consider whether the bishop of Rome had scriptural authority to set himself above other foreign bishops. Elizabeth's Injunctions (1559) had ordered clerics to preach against papal usurpation. If the answer to Cardinal's question was negative, the Protestant Reformation would have a rationale for a return to primitive Christianity.

Philologus, like a good Elizabethan, gives the right response to the crucial question.

> The question is perilous for me to determine,
> Cheifly when the party is judge in the cause;

Yet, if the whole course of Scripture ye examine,
And will be tried by God's holy laws,
Small help shall you find to defend the same cause,
But the contrary may be proved manifestly,
As I in short words will prove to you briefly.   (p. 80)

Wood poses the question so that the "brief" answer would abolish papal claims as well as the whole institution of the papacy when judged by Scripture.

Philologus begins his apology for the Reformation by saying that the pope's claims rest upon the assumption that Peter lived in Rome and that he was charged with the governance of all other disciples. But it cannot be proven, he says, that Peter ever visited Rome, unless one assumes that he intended "Rome" when he wrote from "Babylon." This, he continues, is precisely what certain of the Church Fathers maintained, including Jerome, Augustine, Primatius, and Ambrose, because their writings confirm that Rome is New Babylon. But if this is the case, it would have been better if the Fathers had remained silent, "For they labor to prove Rome by that acception / The whore of Babylon, spoke of in the Revelation" (p. 81).

By a skillful turn in logic, Philologus says that even if Peter ever lived in Rome, it cannot be proven that he was regarded as the "chief" of the disciples. Rather it would be more likely that the "chief" should be the disciple Jesus loved most.

I mean John Evangelist (by birth) cousin-german
To our Saviour Christ, as stories do us tell:
From whose succession if that you should claim
Superiority, you should mend your cause well,
For then of some likelihood of truth it should smell,
Where none so often as Peter was reproved,
Nor from steadfast faith so oftentimes removed.   (p. 81)

But, he continues, suppose that Peter did live in Rome and that he was given preeminence among all other disciples. If so, Peter's successors have very little in common with their original.

Now Peter follows Christ, and all worldly goods forsakes;
But the Pope leaveth Christ, and himself to glory takes.
And to be short, Christ himself refused to be a king,
And the servant above the master may not be;
Which being both true, it is a strange thing,

How the Pope can receive this pomp and dignity,
And yet profess himself Christ's servant to be.
Christ will be no king, the Pope will be more:
The Pope is Christ's master, not his servant, therefore.   (p. 82)

Cardinal listens patiently to these arguments, but he says that they are too "slender" to merit an answer. Wood wants it to appear that Roman Catholics cannot refute such an argument against the papacy and, consequently, they ignore it. A Settlement audience could possibly see the direct confrontation of the New Learning with its critical inquiry and the medieval acceptance of a closed system not subject to human investigation. If so, Wood has hit upon the nerve center of the English Renaissance.

As the trial continues, Cardinal charges the "heretical" Philologus to state his opinion concerning the "holy Sacrament." Philologus paraphrases from the Thirty-nine Articles of the Church of England as he answers,[14]

. . . it is a sign of union,
The which should remain us Christians among,
That one should love another all our life long.
. . . .
The chiefest cause why this Sacrament was ordained,
Was the infirmity of our outward man;
Whereas salvation to all men was proclaimed,
That with true faith apprehend the same can,
By the death of Jesus Christ, that immaculate Lamb;
That the same might the rather of all men be believed,
To the word to add a Sacrament it Christ nothing grieved.   (p. 83)

Referring to the doctrine of transubstantiation, Cardinal asks about the presence of Christ in the Sacrament: "Ah, thou foul heretic! is there bread in the Sacrament? / Where is Christ's body, then, which he did us give?" (p. 84). Philologus answers according to the teaching of the Settlement by insisting upon the mere spiritual presence: "I know to the

---

[14]Article 28 of the Thirty-nine Articles begins as follows: "The Supper of the Lord is not only a sign of the love that Christians ought to have among themselves one to another; but rather it is a Sacrament of our Redemption by Christ's death; insomuch that to such as rightly, worthily, and with faith, receive the same, the Bread which we break is a partaking of the Body of Christ; and likewise the Cup of Blessing is a partaking of the Blood of Christ." *Book of Common Prayer*.

faithful receiver it is there present, / But yet the bread remaineth still, I steadfastly believe" (p. 84).

When Cardinal presses, "In what sense said Christ, *Hoc est corpus meum?*" Philologus shows how different Renaissance hermeneutics were from the medieval.

> Even in the same sense that he said before:
> *Vos estis sal terrae, Vos estis lux mundi,*
> *Ego sum ostium,* and a hundred such more . . .   (p. 84)

Wood thus provides the protagonist with a clever argument against inherited interpretations from Church Fathers. *Hoc est corpus meum* must be interpreted just as the other statements of Jesus are interpreted. Philologus demonstrates his point by questioning Cardinal about other sayings of Christ.

> Were Christ's disciples into salt transformed
> When he said, "Ye are the salt of the earth every one,"
> Or when the light of the world he them affirmed?
> Or himself to be a door when he confirmed?
> Or to be a vine, did his body then change?
> If not then, why now? this to me seemeth strange.   (p. 84)

Such an argument would have been consistent with the method employed by John Colet in his exegesis of the book of Romans at Oxford University, but Cardinal could not accept it even if he had wanted to. The Church Fathers had settled the meaning of Christ's words for all Roman Catholics. Moreover, the Tridentine Profession of Faith (1564), approved by the Council of Trent, had imposed the following restriction against individual interpretation of the Scriptures:

> I acknowledge the sacred Scripture according to that sense which Holy Mother Church has held and holds, to whom it belongs to decide upon the true sense and interpretation of the holy Scriptures, nor will I ever receive and interpret the Scripture except according to the unanimous consent of the Fathers.[15]

The controversy between Philologus and Cardinal over papal jurisdiction versus scriptural interpretation is no real argument at all. Wood,

---

[15]See the full text in Bettenson, 374. The Tridentine Profession of Faith is imposed on all converts to Roman Catholicism to this day.

in the manner of a classical rhetorician, apparently poses the questions through Cardinal in order to expound his polemic from the Settlement point of view. Cardinal could not argue the points in question except from the "orthodox" corpus of inherited beliefs and interpretations handed down from Church Fathers and Councils from one generation to another. The proof, therefore, is all one-sided in favor of the Church of England, since Philologus appeals to an authority that Cardinal cannot recognize. The stalemated theological position cannot be altered until Cardinal is willing to admit that there is a difference between the value of Scripture and the opinions of ecclesiastics. But to do so would necessarily make a "heretic" of Cardinal himself.

Just how far from understanding the critical reasoning of Philologus the cardinal actually is becomes apparent when he concludes the trial.

> This caitiff mine ears with wind he doth fill:
> His words both trust and reason doth want.
> ....
> Nay, if thou beest obstinate, I will say no more.   (p. 85)

Cardinal's only recourse is to ignore the arguments proposed by Philologus, and calling upon Tyranny, he orders his adversary to be placed in prison and tortured by Zeal until a recantation is procured. But, he says, he must not be killed, for "To put him to death would accuse us of tyranny: / But if we could win him, he should do us much honesty" (p. 86).

Philogogus protests that he should not have to be punished for the sake of his conscience, and a recantation would be tantamount to apostasy.

> But in this respect I fear I should kill
> My soul for ever, if against my conscience
> I should to the Pope's laws acknowledge obedience.   (p. 87)

Even when Cardinal threatens to seize his properties, Philologus cites the case of Susanna among the elders and announces, "So will I now spiritual whoredom resist, / And keep me a true virgin to my loving spouse Christ" (p. 89). Curiously, Avarice paraphrases a scriptural text in an effort to convert Philologus:[16] "Wilt thou then neglect the provision of thy household? / Thou art therefore worse than an infidel is" (p. 89). Philologus recognizes the fallacious interpretation of the text and reprimands Avarice for it.

The ultimate thrust of Wood's play comes in the last words of Theologus at the end of act 5. The moral drama designed to move humanity to godliness returns to that theme in a belabored *applicatio*.

> Again, Philologus witnesseth which is the truth of Christ,
> For that consenting to the Pope he did the Lord adjure,
> Whereby he teach the wavering faith on which side to persist:
> And those which have the truth of God, that still they may endure.
>
> (p. 141)

Wood's play is unique in that while he has created a complex situation capable of producing powerful drama, his lack of skill produces an inferior play—tedious and artificial. While the dramatic effect of his use of controversial materials is unimpressive, his polemic is among the best of all such plays. Other Elizabethan interludes that make use of ecclesiastical controversy for similar purposes include: *King Darius*, Lewis Wager's *Life and Repentance of Mary Magdalene*, Ulpian Fulwell's *Like Will to Like*, Thomas Preston's *Cambises*, William Wager's *The Longer Thou Livest the More Fool Thou Art*, *Wealth and Health*, *Godly Queen Hester*, *Albion Knight*, *Trial of Treasure*, *Summer's Last Will and Testament*, *Impatient Poverty*, *The Pedler's Prophecy*, and *New Custom*.

As polemics, Wood's carefully constructed arguments favoring the Settlement position at the expense of Roman Catholicism are as good as most of the tracts and official propaganda. Even more impressive is the close resemblance of Wood's play to a dramatized sermon. While there is little characterization, the allegorical figures, types, and personal characters seem to be reciting lines from a pulpit drama and, like the preacher, quoting scriptural texts in nearly every speech.

If the play fails as drama, it surely succeeds as an *exemplum* supporting the theme of long-suffering and constancy in adversity. Yet, de-

---

[16]Compare 1 Timothy 5:8: "But if any provide not for his own, and specially for those of his own house, he hath denied the faith, and is worse than an infidel." (American Version) It should be noted, however, that like many of the Church Fathers' uses of scriptural texts, this one quoted by the Vice is completely out of context: it is used as a pretext for his own personal design.

spite the popular techniques of Vices in disguise, triumphant boastings, suggestions of devils struggling for souls, a trial scene, and elaborate costuming, the play would have required a histrionic miracle to bring it up to mediocrity.

DRAMA OF THE UNIVERSITY WITS

The young playwrights who revolutionized the history of drama during the years 1585 to 1595 provide some of our best plays before Shakespeare's crowning touch. Elizabethan audiences enjoyed depictions of violence, murders, and executions, as well as allusions to contemporary events. The University Wits drew upon all these to produce enduring works of art.

Certainly one of the most lively topics of their decade was the last desperate struggle of the papacy to reclaim England through foreign invasions by loyal Catholic countries and by subversive activity from within the realm. While specific allusions to the international intrigues are not always recognizable, one can assume that the political crises involving international threats against Protestant England must have helped motivate the national antipathy toward Roman Catholicism in general and Spain in particular.

The University Wits are obviously more concerned with art than with religious controversy, for they had learned that the ecclesiastical materials, like patriotism, could be used to arouse sympathy, emotional response at appropriate instances, or to establish perspective and point of view. Three Wits in particular are worth notice in this regard.

George Peele (1558?-1597), an Oxford man, successful poet, actor, and versatile playwright, created a delightful antiromance comedy in his masterpiece, *The Old Wives' Tale* (c. 1592).[17] Since the play-within-a-play is dependent upon superstitious lore commonly found in old wives' tales, it is possible that the humorous and satirical allusions to Roman Catholic clerics and practices were designed to reinforce the Settlement's view of the Old Faith as mere superstition.

---

[17]The title page of the printed edition (1595) says that the comedy was acted by the Queen's Players, a company organized by Sir Francis Walsingham in 1583 for Elizabeth's special service. The company was dissolved in 1594. References to the play are from the text in C. F. Tucker Brooke and Nathaniel Burton Paradise, eds., *English Drama 1580-1642* (Boston: D. C. Heath and Company, 1933) 25-37.

Yet, the allusions are generally subtle and often mild. For example, when Sacrapant, the evil magician, asks his captive Delia what she would most like to have, she replies,

Then, I pray you, sir, let me have the
best meat from the King of England's table,
and the best wine in all France, brought in by
the veriest knave in all Spain.   (lines 429-432)

The stage directions read, "Enter a Friar with a chine of beef and a pat of wine." To make sure the audience does not miss the thrust at friars, the dialogue spells it out.

Del.:   Is this the veriest knave in all Spain?
Sac.:   Yea.
Del.:   What is he, a friar?
Sac.:   Yea, a friar indefinite, and a knave infinite.   (lines 453-456)

The allusion to friars as knaves is commonplace, dating back to the Middle Ages as a literary convention. However, the reference to Spain, England's enemy and the Roman Catholic defender of the Old Faith as well as the champion of the papacy, is new. A sophisticated audience would have appreciated the allusion, for it strikes at both the political enemy and the most notorious representatives of the Old Faith. Friars had been banished from the realm since the time of Henry VIII's confiscation of the monasteries.

A similar device early in the play is Peele's thrust against the Roman Catholic practice of pilgrimages when the two brothers meet the *senex* Erestus and offer to give him "a palmer's staff of ivory, and a scallop-shell of beaten gold" if they are successful in their mission. Pilgrimages were forbidden by the Settlement,[18] and the absurdity of an ivory palmer's staff is apparent enough, as is the suggestion of a golden scallop shell. Both were to be symbolic of religious devotion and sacrifice, not objects of costly adornment and worldly vanity. The suggestion is that sincere religious devotion was remarkably absent in the Roman Catholic insistence upon pilgrimages. It is significant that Peele mentions the

---

[18]See the "Injunctions of Elizabeth," article 3, in Gee and Hardy, 417-42.

scallop shell as a token of a pious pilgrimage since it was symbolic of a
penitent pilgrimage to the shrine of St. James Compostello in Spain. To
an English audience, Spain was always the champion of Rome.

In another scene, Peele repeats the charge of Reformers against Roman Catholic ecclesiastics and Church officials who administered offices
only for personal profit rather than out of a sense of dedication. In this
instance, Sexton and Churchwarden refuse to bury a dead man because
their fees have not been guaranteed. They reply to their critic,

> Church.: What, would you have us to bury him, and to
> answer it ourselves to the parish?
> Sexton: Parish me no parishes; pay me my fees, and
> let the rest run on in the quarter's accounts,
> and put it down for one of your good deeds,
> o' God's name! for I am not one that curiously
> stands upon merits.   (lines 531-537)

From these examples one realizes that Peele's use of controversial
elements of the religious dispute with Rome is rather mild when compared to Nathaniel Wood's and earlier uses of such materials in Tudor
drama. The same generalization could be made for other plays by Peele
which make use of the religious controversy or which treat Roman Catholic clerics: *Descens Astraeae*, *Edward I*, *The Battle of Alcazar*, and
David and Bethsabe.

Robert Greene (1558-1592), apparently writing for a more popular
audience than Peele, creates in *The Honorable Historie of frier Bacon, and
frier Bongay* (c. 1589) an exemplary romantic comedy. The play testifies
to the Elizabethan fascination with magic and witchcraft, even though
the queen's Injunctions (1559) had forbidden "charms, sorceries, en-
chantments, witchcraft, soothsaying, or any such-like devilish device."
English subjects were forbidden to consult such devices for counsel or
help.

Perhaps it was the love for, or fascination with, the thing forbidden
that kept magic (both black and white) and witchcraft in vogue until the
close of the theatres. Moreover, the references to Roman Catholic practices, such as miraculous powers attributed to saints, holy relics, and
shrines, associated much of the ceremony and ritual of the Old Faith

with superstition of the Middle Ages. It is significant, therefore, that the magician in Greene's play is a friar.

In *Friar Bacon and Friar Bungay*[19] Greene is careful to associate Friar Bacon's occult powers with the devil. In the play, Burden, a doctor at Oxford, reports that all of England and the court of King Henry are saying that Friar Bacon intends to encompass the realm with a wall of brass "by the help of devils and ghastly fiends." Bacon replies that his mystic craft causes the devil himself to tremble.

> The great arch-ruler, potentate of hell,
> Trembles when Bacon bids him or his fiends
> Bow to the force of his pentagonon.
> What art can work, the frolic friar knows;
> And therefore will I turn my magic books,
> And strain out necromancy to the deep.   (1.2.53-58)

When Bacon conjures up the hostess of Henley, it is "*Per omnes deos infernales, Belcephon.*" As a result of Bacon's ability thus to transpose the natural order of things, Bacon's art exposes Doctor Burden as a liar, whereupon he curses the friar significantly, "A pox of all conjuring friars!"

Greene occasionally alludes to customs of the Old Faith, which, although harmless enough in the context of the play, seem to be objectionable to an Elizabethan audience because of the association of Bacon and his art with demonic powers. For example, Prince Edward, in defiance of canonical law, touches upon the practice of lay investiture and possibly on the forbidden practice of simony when he asks the friar to use the black arts to aid him in a love matter. If Bacon is successful, the Prince promises to reward him with ecclesiastical preferment.

> Help, friar, at a pinch, that I may have
> The love of lovely Margaret to myself,
> And, as I am true Prince of Wales, I'll give
> Living and lands to strength thy college state.   (1.5.103-106)

Taking the prince into the inner stage, Bacon tells him,

> Now, frolic Edward, welcome to my cell;
> Here tempers Friar Bacon many toys,

---

[19]References are from the text found in Brooke and Paradise, 71-96.

And holds this place his consistory-court,
Wherein the devils plead homage to his words.   (1.6.1-4)

The association of consistory court with a friar's personal whim and
with the presence of evil spirits is a deliberate perversion of the whole
notion of the consistory; however, from an Elizabethan point of view, the
association of the Roman Catholic consistory with the friar and the devil
would not have been lost upon the audience.

An element of humor enlivens the otherwise solemn scene as Friar
Bungay, with his portace in hand, agrees to perform the marriage ceremony between Edward Lacy and Margaret without parental consent and
without publishing the banns in church. Lacy, the Earl of Lincoln and
friend and confidant of Prince Edward, had obeyed the prince's instruc-
tion by disguising himself as a swain and wooing lovely Margaret, the
park keeper's daughter, on Prince Edward's behalf. Unfortunately for
the prince, Lacy and Margaret fell in love and want to marry before the
prince's return. Prince Edward, observing the scene through a magic
glass at Oxford, calls upon Friar Bacon to stop the wedding by "necro-
mancy" or by powers of devils. Bacon replies, "Fear not, my lord, I'll
stop the jolly friar / From mumbling up his orisons this day" (1.6.152-
153). All at once, Friar Bungay, far away at Fressingfield, becomes mute
and hence unable to proceed with the ceremony. Instead, he merely mut-
ters incoherently, "Hud, hud." Greene makes a further concession to
popular taste by introducing a stock device of the Morality plays: he
causes Bacon to produce a devil to carry Friar Bungay to Oxford on his
back, leaving the lovers unwed. Prince Edward finds the spectacle
amusing.

Bacon, I laugh to see the jolly friar
Mounted upon the devil, and how the earl
Flees with his bonny lass for fear.   (1.6.177-179)

Greene also reflects the Elizabethan disdain and suspicion of secret-
ing one's beauty in a nunnery. Margaret, the fair maid of Fressingfield,
has become a nun after receiving Lacy's letter telling her that he has
been ordered by the king to marry a Spanish lady-in-waiting. When she
comes onstage dressed in her nun's habit, her father laments her rash
decision.

Margaret, be not so headstrong in these vows:
O, bury not such beauty in a cell,
That England hath held famous for the hue!   (1.14.1-3)

But Margaret, unrelenting, expresses a thoroughly medieval point of view—repugnant as it may have been to the spirit of the English Renaissance.

I loved once,—Lord Lacy was my love;
And now I hate myself for that I lov'd.
And doted more on him than on my God;
For this I scourge myself with sharp repents.
But now the touch of such aspiring sins
Tell me all love is lust but love of heavens;
That beauty us'd for love is vanity:
The world contains naught but alluring baits,
Pride, flattery, and inconstant thoughts.
To shun the pricks of death, I leave the world,
And vow to meditate on heavenly bliss,
And live in Framlingham a holy nun,
Holy and pure in conscience and in deed;
And for to wish all maids to learn of me
To seek heaven's joy before earth's vanity.   (1.14.12-26)

Greene reduces these precious protests at once by introducing a ribald thrust, more consonant with Elizabethan notions of nuns. When Lacy and his men arrive at Margaret's house to fetch her to court, they see only Margaret's father and a nun. Ermsby, a gentlemen of the court, assumes that Margaret's father has been familiar with the nun: "The old lecher hath gotten holy mutton to him: a nun, my lord" (1.14.45).

When the true situation is revealed, Lacy expresses his notions of nuns: "What, a malcontent?" Nonetheless, Lacy says that his letter was but a device to try her constancy, and he bids her to leave her "peremptory vows" and marry him. But Margaret replies, "Margaret hath made a vow which may not be revok'd" (1.14.78). Ermsby, in words damaging to Roman Catholic notions of chastity and devotion to God in the state of rigid celibacy, tells Margaret to make an instant decision.

Choose you, fair damsel; yet the choice is yours,—
Either a solemn nunnery or the court,
God or Lord Lacy. Which contents you best,
To be a nun or else Lord Lacy's wife?   (1.14.81-84)

Margaret, forsaking her declaration to be married only to Christ and denying her "irrevocable" vows as a nun, decides in favor of Lacy without a moment's hesitation.

> Off goes the habit of a maiden's heart,
> And, seeing fortune will, fair Framlingham,
> And all the show of holy nuns, farewell!
> Lacy for me, if he will be my lord.   (1.14.89-92)

If the Elizabethan audience enjoyed the mild exposé of a nun's inconstant piety, it certainly would have been amused by a moderately antifeminist, if somewhat bawdy, comment made by Warren, the Earl of Sussex, one of Prince Edward's friends who had up to that moment enjoyed the holiday festivities among the other "frolic courtiers": "To see the nature of women; that / be they never so near God, yet they love to die / in a man's arms" (1.14.103-105).

Meanwhile, Friar Bacon, realizing the folly of his black magic, has broken his "prospective glass," ordered a devil to pursue his scholar Miles, and has determined to spend the rest of his life in penance. On the other hand, Miles suggests that all he needs for his own success as an ecclesiastic are the outward evidences of a scholar.

> I'll take but a book in my hand, a wide-sleeved gown
> on my back, and a crowned cap on my head, and see
> if I can want promotion.   (1.11.142-144)

Miles discovers, however, that the common people are not so easily impressed by his scholar's tags. He comes onstage dressed in academic apparel and says,

> A scholar, quoth you! marry sir, I
> would I had been made a bottle-maker when I
> was made a scholar; for I can get neither to
> be a deacon, reader, nor school- master, no, not
> the clerk of a parish. Some call me dunce;
> another saith, my head is as full of Latin as an
> egg's full of oatmeal.   (1.15.11-17)

Greene may be providing his audience with a general consensus of Elizabethan opinion concerning the pointless absurdities and theological subtleties associated with the medieval scholastics.

Greene disposes of Miles by having another devil appear onstage with the promise to make the former Oxford scholar a tapster in hell.

Returning to the popular device, he causes Miles to mount the devil's back and spur his way to hell: "O Lord, here's even a goodly marvel, / when a man rides to hell on the devil's back!" (1.15.75-76).

Friar Bacon and Friar Bungay uses the trappings and attitudes of the Old Faith to create atmosphere, but the total effect is innocuous. There are no polemics, and the elements of ecclesiastical controversy do not detract from the art.

On the other hand, an Elizabethan audience could not fail to make the necessary connection between the Old Faith and medieval superstition, ignorance, and superficial piety. The friars of the play are always spoken of as "jolly," and they prove to be meddlesome in things which ordinarily should not have been their business. But even so, their function in the drama is not to damage the Roman Catholic faith but to provide good comedy at the expense of Roman Catholics. Greene's use of religious controversy effects a gay spectacle for a popular audience without necessarily calling attention to materials drawn from the dispute with Rome. Greene's other plays that use ecclesiastical controversy or portray clerics include: *Alphonsus of Aragon*, *Orlando Furioso*, possibly *George-a-Greene*, and *James the Fourth*.

Of all the University Wits, Christopher Marlowe (1564-1593) is the most consistently vehement in his dramatic derogation of Roman Catholics. Yet, he is at the same time the most brilliant and talented of the group. For these reasons one can expect an uncommon performance from a dramatist in whom such elements are combined. The reports of his "good service" to the queen, possibly as an espionage agent against Jesuit missionaries, are well known.

The Jew of Malta (c. 1589)[20] was Marlowe's most popular drama among Elizabethan audiences. It contains sufficient examples to demonstrate the playwright's use of controversial materials and to determine his strongly Protestant bias at a time when the Spanish Armada was still fresh in the minds of Elizabethan citizens.

It is significant that the Prologue is spoken by "Machiavel." Not only does Machiavel offer a mild thrust against the pope, but he sets the tone for the tragedy to follow. He suggests that Roman Catholics really employ Machiavellian policy, though they deny it.

---

[20]References are to the text in Brooke and Paradise, 195-224.

Though some speak openly against my books,
Yet will they read me, and thereby attain
To Peter's chair; and when they cast me off,
Are poison'd by my climbing followers.   (10-13)

Moreover, Machiavellian policy, as Elizabethans understood it, is contrary to the humanistic ideals of the period, as Machiavel confesses.

I count religion but a childish toy,
And hold there is no sin but ignorance.
. . . .
Might first made kings, and laws were then most sure
When, like the Draco's, they were writ in blood.   (14-15, 20-21)

Machiavel announces that a rich Jew gained his great wealth from following Machiavellian policy; consequently, the Jew must not be judged adversely simply because he, like those aspiring perhaps to Peter's chair, "favours" Machiavel.

Act 1 shows Barabas, the rich Jew of Malta, musing over his great riches. He explains that no one nowadays is honored unless he is wealthy. Better it is to be a rich Jew than a poor Christian. Moreover, Christians are hypocrites, for they profess one thing and do another.

For I can see no fruits in all their faith,
But malice, falsehood, and excessive pride,
Which methinks fits not their profession.   (1.1.115-117).

When three other Jews enter and report the arrival of the Turks on the coasts of Malta, Barabas further reveals his Machiavellian character: "Nay, let 'em [i.e., Turks] combat, conquer, and kill all, / So they spare me, my daughter, and my wealth" (1.1.151-152).

Calling upon his daughter Abigail to help him extract the concealed treasure from his confiscated mansion—now converted into a Christian convent—he tells her to apply to the abbess for admission to their order as a nun.

Ay, daughter, for religion
Hides many mischiefs from suspicion.   (1.2.282-283)
. . . .
A counterfeit profession is better
Than unseen hypocrisy.   (1.2.292-293)

Abigail obediently goes about her father's business and encounters three friars and two nuns. She tells the abbess that she wishes to live a life "in penitence" and to become a novice in their nunnery "to make atonement for my labouring soul." Marlowe prepares for a little salacious humor later by allowing the two friars a brief *double entendre*.

1 Friar: No doubt, brother, but his proceedeth of the spirit.
2 Friar: Ay, and a moving spirit too, brother; but come,
    Let us entreat she may be entertain'd.   (1.2.326-328)

And Barabas, pretending to be outraged by his daughter's "mortification," says, "I charge thee on my blessing that thou leave / These devils, and their damned heresy" (1.2.344-345).

    Don Mathias, a gentleman, expresses the Elizabethan repugnance to beautiful women in nunneries similar to that in *Friar Bacon and Friar Bungay*. In the lusty spirit of comic irreverence, Mathias says of Abigail,

Tut, she were fitter for a tale of love,
Than to be tired out with orisons;
And better would she far become a bed,
Embraced in a friendly lover's arms,
Than rise at midnight to a solemn mass.   (1.2.367-371)

    In act 2, Barabas is able to purchase another house with treasure extracted by his daughter from its place of hiding in the nunnery, and he has reclaimed Abigail from the nuns. But as his desire for vengeance upon Christians for their apparent injustice against him increases, Barabas further makes of Abigail a pawn for his personal ambitions by causing her to pretend to return the love declarations of Lodowick, son of the governor. At the same time, he tells Mathias, Abigail's true love, that Lodowick forces his attentions upon Abigail. Trying to create as much dissension as possible between the two men, Barabas tells Lodowick that Mathias plans to kill his rival for Abigail's affections. Then, Barabas tells Abigail that she must deceive Lodowick by pretending to accept his betrothal.

    When one hears Barabas's rationale for such an act of deception, it seems to suggest the Elizabethan understanding of Jesuit subversives in England. Marlowe was well acquainted with Jesuit practices before and after the critical year of the Armada. That is, Elizabethans complained that Jesuits took oaths of allegiance to the queen, knowing that when an opportunity arose to effect their grand conspiracy they were not compelled to keep their oaths. Consequently, deception was permissible for

Jesuits in England because they were not obliged to keep oaths made to
"heretics." If Marlowe had anything of the sort in his mind, the following
words spoken by Barabas to his daughter would have made the passage
more relevant to the times and more meaningful to the audience.

> It's no sin to deceive a Christian;
> For they themselves hold it a principle,
> Faith is not to be held with heretics . . .   (2.3.315-317)

Ithimore, Barabas's villainous slave, provides Marlowe with an opportunity to associate friars and nuns with lechery. Ithimore presumptuously asks Abigail a very "feeling" question: " . . . have not the nuns
fine sport with the friars / now and then?" (3.3.37-38). Ithimore reflects
the common Reformation attitude toward nuns and friars. One recalls,
for example, Henry VIII's Dissolution of the Lesser Monasteries (1536)
wherein monks, canons, and nuns were accused of "carnal and abominable living."

Ignoring Ithimore's ribald jest, Abigail orders him to fetch one of the
friars at the "new-made nunnery" so that she might speak with him.
When Friar Jacomo, a French Dominican, arrives, Abigail solicits his
help in gaining admission to the order of nuns. She explains,

> My sinful soul, alas, hath pac'd too long
> The fatal labyrinth of misbelief,
> Far from the Sun that gives eternal life.   (3.3.69-71)

After Barabas learns that Abigail has become a nun in earnest, he
seeks revenge upon her and all nuns of the order by causing Ithimore to
take a bowl of poisoned rice to the nunnery. The nuns eat the poisoned
food and become mortally ill. They send for the friars to hear their last
confessions.

Abigail comes onstage, also mortally ill, and makes her confession to
Friar Bernardine. During confession she reveals the guilt of her father
in arranging the deaths of her two rivals, but she implores her "ghostly
father" to reveal the secret of her confession to no one. The friar replies
sanctimoniously,

> Know that confession must not be reveal'd.
> The canon law forbids it, and the priest
> That makes it known, being degraded first,
> Shall be condemn'd, and then sent to the fire.   (3.6.33-36)

Abigail's last words before she dies are solemn and pious: "Convert my father that he may be sav'd / And witness that I die a Christian" (3.6.39-40). But Marlowe reduces the otherwise sad moment to a vulgar scene when the friar reveals his lascivious nature by responding to the dead nun's last words, "Ah, and a virgin too; that grieves me most" (3.6.41). Making a mockery of the canonical law forbidding him to repeat what he has heard in confession, the depraved friar further reveals his covetousness and avarice by saying, "But I must to the Jew and exclaim on him, / And make him stand in fear of me" (3.6.42-43).

Just then Friar Jacomo enters and says that all of the nuns of the order are dead, but Friar Bernadine is so anxious to blackmail Barabas that he will bury only Abigail before going to the Jew. The others will have to remain unburied until that more important task is completed.

It is possible that in this scene Marlowe is exposing two Roman Catholic institutions at once, both of which were particularly objectionable to Elizabethans: friars and confession. Yet, neither depraved friars nor abuse of the confessional were new to the drama. Marlowe seems to stir up more than a humorous disregard for the unworthy ecclesiastics of the Old Faith. Instead, he generates an effective hostility towards such representatives of the Holy Church who apparently hold nothing sacred, not even the canonical laws to which they are committed. Still, unworthy as the friars may be, their activities are consonant with Machiavellian policy by which they may climb to Peter's chair.

Act 4 begins with a continuation of the suggestion of lechery associated with those in regular orders. Ithimore says that since the nuns are dead, he should now kill the monks as well. But Barabas answers that such a measure will be unncessary: "Thou shalt not need, for now the nuns are dead, / They'll die with grief" (4.1.16-17).

Barabas is rejoicing in the knowledge of his daughter's death when the two friars enter. Ithimore irreverently refers to them as "two religious caterpillars," and Barabas adds his own antipathy by commenting, "I smelt 'em ere they came."

Marlowe depicts the scene with a clever touch of humor as the friars attempt to blackmail Barabas. But when Barabas discovers their rascality, he has a trick of his own—he pretends conversion.

O holy friars,the burthen of my sins
Lie heavy on my soul; then pray you tell me,

Is't not too late now to turn Christian?
I have been zealous in the Jewish faith,
Hard-hearted to the poor, a covetous wretch,
That would for lucre's sake have sold my soul.
. . . .
I am a Jew, and therefore am I lost.
Would penance serve for this my sin,
I could afford to whip myself to death.   (4.1.51-56, 60-62).

Ithimore also pretends conversion, and joining the absurd confession of his master, he comments, "And so could I; but penance will not serve" (4.1.63).

Barabas knows just how to motivate the friars into accepting his "conversion" and continues to recite well-known acts of penance practiced by the Old Faith, "To fast, to pray, and wear a shirt of hair, / And on my knees creep to Jerusalem" (4.1.64-65). Moreover, Barabas offers a long catalogue of treasures and merchandise in various parts of the earth, including money in the bank: "All this I'll give to some religious house, / So I may be baptiz'd, and live therein" (4.1.78-79).

With a skillful allusion to the rivalry among religious orders, particularly among friars, Barabas thus initiates strife between the two contending ecclesiastics as each attempts to persuade Barabas to join his respective order. An uproariously comical scene follows in which the Jew agrees to go with one and then with the other, while each one points out the disadvantages of joining the other. The argument ends with the friars fighting each other—a device that Heywood used effectively between two ecclesiastics in *The Pardoner and the Friar*.

When Friar Bernardine leaves the stage, accompanied by Ithimore, Barabas tells Friar Jacomo, in a clever stroke of irony, that he will join the Jacobins.

Why, brother, you converted Abigail;
And I am bound in charity to requite it,
And so I will.   (4.1.109-111).

Adding absurdity to the already ridiculous scene, Barabas says that the Turk shall be one of his godfathers. However, once the friars have left the stage, Barabas lets it be known to the audience that he has no intention of leaving the pleasures of this life to "fast and be well whipp'd." He has a better plan: he intends to murder the friars.[21]

After the second friar has been turned over to the authorities and executed as a part of Barabas's design, Ithimore returns with a humorous account of the knave's death.

> I never knew a man take his death so
> patiently as this friar. He was ready to leap off
> ere the halter was about his neck; and when
> the hangman had put on his hempen tippet, he
> made such haste to his prayers as if he had
> had another cure to serve. . . .   (4.2.26-31)

It is a good finish for the depraved friars.

Marlowe thus uses the depraved clerics to provide some of the necessary humor for his tragedy. In doing so, he is merely following the medieval convention of abusing friars for their worldliness, greed, hypocrisy, and lechery. By making the Jew a perceptive stranger, outside the machinations of the Holy Church, he is able to provide a point of view critical of the Old Faith which would otherwise have been impossible without running the risk of calling attention to it and thus detracting from his art. While many elements of the religious controversy are used to provide atmosphere for the lively action onstage, they are so carefully blended that they seldom call attention to themselves.

Marlowe's particular vitriolic satire comes through, however, in some of his other plays, although it is not as well sustained nor as consistent as it is in *The Jew of Malta*. For example, one of the most caustic, and still humorous, depictions of the pope comes through in *Faustus* in the scene at the Vatican Palace. *Edward II* deals with the whole problem of ecclesiastics and their contempt for royal juridsiction, particularly in act 1 where the bishop of Coventry defies his temporal lord. *The Massacre at Paris* is thoroughly hostile to the Old Faith. But Marlowe's

---

[21]An amusing incident follows in which Barabas and Ithimore strangle one friar and prop his body up against a post. The second friar comes at the appointed hour, sees the first friar, resumes the altercation, strikes him down, and assumes that he has killed him. But since the incident is generally regarded as a later addition to the play by Heywood, it is not discussed here. The story of the two friars appears in two of Heywood's works, although it derives ultimately from a novella of Masuccio.

strength is in his humorous, and thus indirect, attack upon the Roman Catholic customs and practices.

The University Wits used materials of the religious controversy in their plays, but the strong polemical force practically disappeared. To be sure, the old hostility was still a powerful undercurrent, but the necessity for Reformation and Settlement apologetics was remarkably absent. By the time of their writing, there seemed to have been a more conscious desire to create good theatre than effective propaganda. The plays that endured rank with the best of Renaissance drama; even Shakespeare learned from the Wits.

Peele, Greene, and Marlowe seemed to represent Roman Catholicism in terms of contemporary Elizabethan attitudes towards the Old Faith. That is, they tended to relate Romanist practices and ecclesiastics with superstition, ignorance (a major sin for the Renaissance), corruption, covetousness, and hypocrisy. Yet, the satire, when it occurred, was generally mild and innocuous. The University Wits learned to use the materials of the controversy the way any other materials must be used in effective dramatic art—to provide a point of view, to create atmosphere, to enhance the dramatic situation, and to provide an aid for convincing imitation. Using all of these techniques, the University Wits provided a major step in the history of dramatic art.

CHAPTER VI

SHAKESPEARE'S USE
OF RELIGIOUS CONTROVERSY
IN *KING JOHN*

Shakespeare was too much an artist and too much a businessman to make himself vulnerable to either the antitheatre officials in London or the anti-Romanist agents at Court. He wrote for a popular audience and was completely dependent upon the pleasure of that general public during the last decade of the sixteenth century. It seems unlikely, therefore, that Shakespeare would have used the stage to support his private notions about religion. At first he seemed more interested in reflecting public taste, not in prescribing it.

Like other successful dramatists of his period, Shakespeare held the mirror up to not only nature but also contemporary attitudes, including the instinctive religious beliefs of his audience. That mirror reflected the attitudes and fears generated by the recent, infamous Spanish Armada and its resultant surge of anti-Roman Catholic hostility in the name of patriotism.

Hostility against Roman Catholic subversive activity reached an apex in 1591 when Elizabeth issued a proclamation against Jesuit missionary priests. Two years later the hostility against all Roman Catholics was so pronounced that Parliament passed the Act Against Recusants.

The Preamble of that document reflects the official view concerning Roman Catholics in England.

> For the better discovering and avoiding of all such traitorous and most dangerous conspiracies and attempts as are daily devised and practiced against our most gracious sovereign lady the queen's majesty and the happy estate of this commonweal, by sundry wicked and seditious persons, who, terming themselves Catholics, and being indeed spies and intelligencers, not only for her majesty's foreign enemies, but also for rebellious and traitorous subjects born within her highness's realms and dominions, and hiding their most detestable and devilish purposes under a false pretext of religion and conscience, do secretly wander and shift from place to place within this realm, to corrupt and seduce her majesty's subjects, and to stir them to sedition and rebellion. . . . [1]

The act, in short, provided that every English subject older than the age of sixteen, "being a popish recusant" and refusing to attend divine services of the Church of England, would be restricted to his place of residence, from which he was forbidden to travel more than a distance of five miles.

An anonymous play entitled *Troublesome Reign of King John* was printed in 1591, right in the midst of general anti-Roman Catholic hostility. It is as vitriolic as Bale's play. It was also in the midst of anti-Roman Catholic hostility that Shakespeare wrote his own *King John*, and for the same audience as the anonymous play. Since the days of Henry VIII's reformation of the Church of England, the historical King John had been regarded as a champion of English kings against the usurpation of Roman bishops. If Shakespeare did not have his fingers upon the pulse of the nation, it is impossible to explain why he chose such a subject as King John for a play at all.

It has been customary to say that Shakespeare's *King John* is a condensation of the anonymous *Troublesome Reign*, and that Shakespeare's play was written sometime during the years 1594-1597. But one editor, E. A. J. Honigmann, in the new Arden edition (1954), argues for an earlier date, 1590 or 1591. That would mean, of course, that Shakespeare's play would have had no necessary relationship to the *Troublesome Reign*, and that the *Troublesome Reign* could have been an expansion of Shakespeare's original. In view of the evidence we now have, there is as much

---

[1] See "Act Against Recusants," in Gee and Hardy, 498-508.

to favor Honigmann's view as the traditional one. Should the earlier date theory prevail, all of the scholarship based upon Shakespeare's omission or toning down of the Roman Catholic derogation contained in the *Troublesome Reign* would have to be reevaluated.

Since placing a date on the writing of *King John* is an impossibility in view of present evidence, it seems far more beneficial to read Shakespeare's play without reference to the *Troublesome Reign*. And, of course, by reading *King John* as a self-contained whole, one is left with what is most desirable: Shakespeare's writing.

Shakespeare's *The Life and Death of King John*,[2] unlike most of the Tudor drama in which the religious controversy plays a significant part, successfully avoids many individual grievances of Protestants against Catholics by sustaining the essentially Anglican point of view in matters of church and state that had been brought down in history from the time of William the Conqueror. That is, in the controversy between England and Rome, neither the English Church nor the English nation was to be dominated by foreign powers.

Shakespeare, with remarkable restraint when one considers the anti-Roman Catholic temper during the period of the play's composition, presents the bitter conflict as a matter of politics rather than merely a religious quarrel. Consequently, he raises certain questions in the drama which lift the entire problem above the vitriolic charges and counter-charges for which the sixteenth century is noted.

The questions Shakespeare raises in *King John* are these: Does a king rule his dominions by the grace of God or by the grace of the pope? Does a *de facto* king have the right to expect absolute loyalty and obedience from his subjects, even when his right to the succession is questionable? Is rebellion against the king ever justifiable, even when the king proves to be wicked and an enemy of the Church? Do foreign princes have the right to interfere with a Christian king's administration of his own dominions? Having been raised to hear questions such as these resolved by the enforced preaching of the *Book of Homilies*, Shakespeare's audience would have known the right answer to a man. Further, official censor-

---

[2]References to the play are to the text in G. B. Harrison, ed., *Shakespeare: The Complete Works* (New York: Harcourt, Brace, and World, 1952) 547-78.

ship would have guaranteed the correct response by dramatists in their plays.

When Shakespeare stresses the political nature of the religious dispute with Rome, he is writing within the range of a wide historical background, thoroughly familiar to the audience during the last decade of the century. It is no accident, therefore, that *King John* begins with allusions to the question of usurpation. While the king may have succeeded by "borrowed Majesty," the problem of usurpation is dealt with on several levels as a recurring theme throughout the play.

From an Anglican point of view, however, the most detestable usurpation was perpetrated by the Roman papacy. One recalls that the queen had begun her reign upon the assumption that the popes had usurped ancient royal prerogatives by interfering with the internal affairs of England's citizens and her Church. Elizabeth's Act of Supremacy (1559) abolished all papal jurisdiction in England, so that "all usurped and foreign power and authority, spiritual and temporal" could be removed forever.[3] Her Royal Injunctions (1559) began by ordering all ecclesiastics to preach sermons against papal usurpation. It need not be surprising to learn that homilies and propaganda tracts of the period coupled the name of the pope with usurpation.

If English subjects were not convinced already, Pope Pius V's bull excommunicating and deposing Elizabeth (1570) reinforced the charge of usurpation. In that document Pius referred to himself as "chief over all nations and all kingdoms, to pluck up, destroy, scatter, dispose, plant and build . . . "[4] The presence of the papal legate, Cardinal Pandulph, onstage would have been a sufficient reminder to Shakespeare's audience that the question of Rome's usurpation was still a live issue.

In act 3 Shakespeare implicitly raises the question of whether a king rules in his own right by the grace of God, or whether he rules by permission of the pope. Pandulph, as legate from Rome, demands to know why King John defies the Holy Church by refusing to admit Stephen Langton, the pope's choice for England's archbishop of Canterbury. John answers as Henry VIII or Elizabeth would have answered: "What

---

[3]See the "Supremacy Act of Elizabeth," in Bettenson, 332-33.

[4]See "*Regnans in excelsis*," in Bettenson, 340-41.

earthly name to interrogatories / Can task the free breath of a sacred king?" (3.1.147-148).

Ironically, Pandulph had made his entrance by addressing King John and King Philip of France as "you anointed deputies of Heaven!" Perhaps without realizing it, Pandulph gives lip service to the divine right of kings, while his message from the pope would seem to deny that right. It may be recalled that John Bale's *King John* had centered the stage action upon this very point: a king was God's anointed minister to rule over his people. As such, he was answerable to no other power under heaven. Henry's assumption of the title "Supreme Head" (1531) was an affirmation of the right to rule his own dominions in matters spiritual and temporal, answerable to God alone. Elizabeth recognized her function as "Supreme Governor as well in all spiritual or ecclesiastical things or causes, as temporal." Political tracts and certain official homilies had stressed the point that kings, whether good or evil, reigned by divine sanction. Consequently, when John answers the cardinal, his words carry the whole force of the English understanding of a king's divine right to rule his dominions without interference from any foreign power, temporal or spiritual.

John's antipapal remarks can be seen, within the context of the times, not as being derogatory to the Roman Catholic Church but as an expression of the Reformation position. That position sees the pope as merely the bishop of Rome and an Italian priest with no more legal rights in the king's dominions than any other ecclesiastic.

> Thou canst not, Cardinal, devise a name
> So slight, unworthy, and ridiculous
> To charge me to an answer, as the Pope.
> Tell him this tale; and from the mouth of England
> Add thus much more: that no Italian priest
> Shall tithe or toll in our dominions,
> But as we, under Heaven, are supreme head,
> So under Him that great supremacy,
> Where we do reign, we will alone uphold
> Without the assistance of a mortal hand.
> So tell the Pope, all reverence set apart
> To him and his usurped authority.   (3.1.149-160)

The point is clear: John assumes the Anglican position that his authority to reign is independent of the pope's claims to the contrary. As

Supreme Head of the Church in England, John does not require assistance from the pontiff. As Supreme Head he also retains Edward the Confessor's precedents of investing his own primate and administering ecclesiastical affairs in the national Church. Elizabeth had demonstrated her position when she wrote to Dr. Richard Cox, bishop of Ely, demanding his conformity: "You know what you were before I made you what you are now. If you do not immediately comply with my requests, I will unfrock you, by God."[5] Elizabeth did not unfrock Archbishop Grindal, but when he refused to comply with her wishes, she placed him under house arrest for five years and assumed his duties personally. Thus, John does not reply to Cardinal Pandulph as a spiritual subject of the Roman See, but as a "sacred king" who is subject only to God. Whenever the bishop of Rome attempts to interfere with this normal state of affairs, he does so by "usurped authority."

The whole issue became clear in the Restraint of Appeals Act (1533) in which the king of England is referred to as the embodiment of ancient power, under whom "spiritualty and temporalty, be bounden and ought to bear, next to God, a natural and humble obedience," for he rules by the sufferance of Almighty God and without restraint from any foreign powers. The act reiterates the statutes of the realm passed during the reigns of Edward I, Edward III, Richard II, Henry IV, and others, in an effort to preserve ancient royal prerogatives from the "annoyance" of the Roman See as well as "other foreign potentates."[6]

The important First Act of Succession (1534) began with the explanation that such legislation is necessary because "the Bishop of Rome, and see apostolic, contrary to the great and inviolable grants of jurisdictions given by God immediately to emperors, kings, and princes, in succession to their heirs, has presumed, in times past, to invest who should please them, to inherit in other men's kingdoms and dominions."[7] Significantly, the act acknowledged England as "an imperial realm," in which Henry VIII maintained the status of any other emperor: "*rex est imperator in regno suo.*" Clearly, Shakespeare's audience

---

[5] G. B. Harrison, ed., *The Letters of Queen Elizabeth* (London: Cassel and Company, 1935) 121.

[6] See "Restraint of Appeals," in Gee and Hardy, 187-95.

[7] See the "First Act of Succession," in Gee and Hardy, 232-43.

was prepared to share in King John's reply to Cardinal Pandulph and would have maintained that the king rules in his dominions without prerequisite permission from Rome.

King Philip probably represents a standard Roman Catholic response to John's bold defiance of papal jurisdiction: "Brother of England, you blaspheme in this" (3.1.161). After all, Pope Boniface VIII's famous *Unam Sanctam* bull (1302) was still in force as a reminder to loyal Roman Catholics that "it is altogether necessary to salvation for every human creature to be subject to the Roman pontiff."[8] Thus when King John derogates the papal office, he also defies the sacred decisions of Church Councils and popes over the course of several centuries.

But King John deviates from the general principle under discussion and alludes to certain objectionable features of Roman Catholic practices in a manner not characteristic of Shakespeare at his best. John answers Philip's charge:

> Though you and all the kings of Christendom
> Are led so grossly by this meddling priest,
> Dreading the curse that money may buy out,
> And by the merit of vile gold, dross, dust,
> Purchase corrupted pardon of a man
> Who in that sale sells pardon from himself,
> Though you and all the rest so grossly led
> This juggling witchcraft with revenue cherish,
> Yet I alone, alone do me oppose
> Against the Pope and count his friends my foes.   (3.1.162-171)

Pardons and indulgences were among the chief objects of Luther's attack upon the Church, and they remained the objects of abuse and satire throughout the century. In John's derogation of the "meddling priest," the commonplace ridicule of the "curse that money may buy out" is not unlike similar attacks reflected in stage plays during the polemical period of the English Reformation. Elizabethans of the Settlement period would have understood John's implication of the Reformation position that while pardons may be purchased, it is for the profitable market of man and not sanctioned by Scripture, for only God has the power to pardon sin. Moreover, the allusion to indulgences as a part of "juggling witchcraft" is little different from official statutes of the

---

[8]See the excerpt from *Unam Sanctam*, in Bettenson, 161-63.

realm which never seemed to tire of associating Roman Catholic practices with superstition.

The inclusion of such allusions at this point is further evidence of how closely Shakespeare reflects the attitudes of the Elizabethan Settlement of Religion. The audience may have seen John's solitary position among the temporal sovereigns of Europe as essentially the position of England during the period of the Counter-Reformation. For Shakespeare's audience, Elizabeth alone of the reigning princes was not "grossly led" by "witchcraft" to fill the coffers of Rome. Recent plots against the government not only placed English Roman Catholics under official surveillance as potential traitors, but almost of necessity "friends" of the pope became "foes" of the Protestant queen's government. Thus, John's anachronistic position had particular relevance for Shakespeare's audience because John's reply reflects precise English attitudes of the Reformation.

A second question Shakespeare's play raises demanded considerably more delicacy in handling on the stage: Does a *de facto* king have the right to expect absolute loyalty, even when his right to the succession is questionable? It required particular delicacy on Shakespeare's part because of the very tenuous claim to succession by the House of Tudor.

In the play, France accuses John of disregarding the natural order of succession by usurping the throne with utter disregard for Prince Arthur's more immediate right to the succession. John vindicates his role by implying that might makes right, "Our strong possession and our right for us" (1.1.39). Queen Mother Elinor responds to this significantly, "Your strong possession much more than your right, / Or else it must go wrong with you and me" (1.1.40-41). When Elinor and Constance debate the relative merits of the right of succession, Elinor says, " . . . Thou unadviséd scold, I can produce / A will that bars the title of thy son" (2.1.191-192).

Thus far the problem is one which no doubt had occurred to Shakespeare's audience. Not only had the right of the Scottish line been overlooked in the English succession, but Mary Stuart had bypassed her own son, by terms of her will, in favor of Philip II of Spain as heir apparent. Moreover, while Cardinal Pandulph's quarrel with John is not at first directly concerned with his "usurpation" or his right to succeed to the throne, Pope Pius V's *Regnans in excelsis* (1570), excommunicating and deposing Elizabeth, had expressed the common Romanist position that

Elizabeth was not the rightful successor to the throne. Pius's bull deprived the queen "of her pretended right to the aforesaid realm."

The first Tudor king had solved the problem about his right to succession, even when there remained the possibility of Yorkist heirs more immediate in the line of succession. Henry VII helped secure his position on the throne by a marriage with a descendant of Edward IV, and in 1495 he led Parliament to enact legislation making it no treason to obey a *de facto* king. John seems to share the Tudor point of view by asking a most significant question, "Doth not the crown of England prove the King?" (2.1.273).

The problem of a dubious access to the throne can not justify the attitude assumed by the citizens of Angiers. They will not recognize King John nor obey him until they are assured that he is the rightful king: ". . . but he that proves the King, / To him will we prove loyal" (2.1.270-271).

An Elizabethan audience would probably have felt that France's "usurpation" of England's right to obey a crowned king was, as it proved to be in the case of Lewis, a mere pretext for personal gain. By the same token, Roman Catholic charges that England's queen had no right to rule would probably have impressed the audience as being a variation on the same theme, except in this case for the personal advantage of the pope.

At any rate, the fact that a king ruled in England by sanction of the Parliament should have been sufficient to answer the question about dubious rights to succession, and this had been the most effective means of answering those who pressed Mary Stuart's claims.

A third question raised by Shakespeare's play provides more effective dramatic possibilities: Is rebellion against the king ever justifiable, even when the king proves to be wicked and an enemy of the Church? No matter how much Englishmen may have changed their point of view on this question before the year 1649 when King Charles I was beheaded by Parliamentary consent, Shakespeare's audience had been instructed over a long period of time in the doctrine that rebellion against the prince was among the gravest sins imaginable. It was a part of the doctrine of Tudor absolutism.

The most relevant part of the rebellion theme occurs in act 3 when Cardinal Pandulph excommunicates King John.

Then, by the lawful power that I have,
Thou shalt stand cursed and excommunicate.
And blessèd shall he be that doth revolt
From his allegiance to an heretic;
And meritorious shall that hand be called,
Canónizéd and worshipped as a saint,
That takes away by any secret course
Thy hateful life.   (3.1.172-179)

Actually, such a charge against Roman Catholic policy had been at the
heart of several plots to assassinate the queen, even extending to late in
the century. For example, as late as 1594 one Hugh Cahill, an Irishman,
is reported to have confessed voluntarily "that when at Brussels, Father
Holt and others said it would be a most blessed thing to kill the Queen,
as by it he would win Heaven, and become a saint if he should be killed;
he that would do it would be chronicled for ever."[9]

Sir Edward Coke, solicitor general, described a number of Roman
Catholic attempts to incite rebellion and kill the queen.

> To this end many needy and desperate young men are seduced by Jesuits
> and seminary priests with great rewards and promises to kill the Queen,
> being persuaded that it is glorious and meritorious, and that if they die
> in this action, they will inherit Heaven and be canonized as saints.[10]

Two pamphlets written probably by Cardinal Allen for distribution
upon the occasion of the Spanish invasion (1588) are significant for the
light they bring to this dark business. The first calls Elizabeth "an in-
cestuous bastard, begotten and born in sin of an infamous courtesan,"
and it calls upon Roman Catholics in England to rise up in arms against
the "infamous, depraved, accursed, excommunicate heretic."[11] The second, called *Declaration*, calls for the "deprivation and deposition" of the
queen in the pope's name, and for those who help to capture "the said

---

[9]G. B. Harrison, *Elizabethan Journals* (Ann Arbor: University of Michigan Press, 1955) 288.

[10]Harrison, 289.

[11]Philip Hughes, *The Reformation in England* (London: Hollis and Carter, 1950) 3:380.

usurper or any of her accomplices," Plenary Indulgence is to be allowed.[12]

The point of view expressed in Allen's pamphlets is reinforced by Pope Gregory XIII's license for political assassination. Gregory had told a group of assassins that "whoever sends 'the Queen' out of the world with the pious intention of doing God service . . . gains merit."[13] Other allegations of ecclesiastical sanction of the assassination of Elizabeth are recorded by Holinshed in connection with various conspiracies centered around Mary Stuart's claims to the throne.[14]

The question of rebellion seems to fascinate Shakespeare. In the play, Pandulphus calls upon English citizens in the name of His Holiness to rebel against an heretical king. On the other hand, John Bale's thesis was that citizens never have a right to rebel, even when the king may be wicked, for rebellion against God's anointed minister is tantamount to rebellion against God Himself. Shakespeare seems to champion this doctrine in his plays, although it would have been practically impossible for him to have done otherwise in view of the vigilance of official censors.

The Northern Rebellion (1569) may have prompted the addition of the important homily "Against Disobedience and Wilful Rebellion" (1571) in the official *Book of Homilies*. It would have been difficult for any man in Shakespeare's audience to have escaped hearing this homily many times during his lifetime. Yet the homily is little more than a sum

---

[12]Hughes, 3:381.

[13]E. I. Watkin, *Roman Catholicism in England from the Reformation to 1950* (London: Oxford University Press, 1957) 37.

[14]For example, the celebrated case of Dr. William Parry's treason produced as evidence the following letter from Cardinal di Como in Rome, dated 30 January 1584: "Monsignor, the Sanctity of our Lordship first has read the letters of your Lordship in full faith and cannot but praise the good disposition you profess towards the public welfare, for which his Sanctity exhorts you to persevere so that you might attain the ends that your Lordship promises. In order that you may be further assisted by that good spirit which moved you, he grants you his blessing and full forgiveness of all sins, as your Lordship has requested, assuring that besides the reward that your Lordship will have in heaven his Sanctity will also put himself in your debt recognizing the merits of your Lordship in the best manner, and so much more so because your Lordship shows great modesty in expecting nothing. So carry out your saintly and honored intentions and be well. Finally I offer you from my heart and wish you every good and happy success." Holinshed, 4:573. Translated from the Italian by Frida A. Norman, professor of Italian, Georgia State University, Atlanta GA.

mation of absolutist doctrine extending from the first Tudor king and re-
iterated by statesmen and ecclesiastics of the New Faith for most of the
century.[15] The homily repeats the point from Paul's epistle to the Romans that Bale's *King John* had expressed: "The powers that be are ordained of God. Whosoever therefore resisteth the power, resisteth the
ordinance of God: and they that resist shall receive to themselves damnation" (Romans 13:1-2). The scriptural passage goes on to say that even
wicked kings rule according to God's will and must be obeyed as though
they were good. The homily further maintains that Satan is the author
of rebellion.

The homily "Against Disobedience and Wilful Rebellion" discusses
the possibility that the king may prove to be an enemy of the Church,
and if he does, what should be the attitude of his subjects toward obeying
his will? In the play, Cardinal Pandulph has stated the attitude of the papacy just as clearly as Pope Pius V had stated it in *Regnans in excelsis*:
subjects are absolved from oaths of loyalty in such a case, and they are
forbidden to obey an heretical sovereign. In 1580, however, Pope Gregory XIII qualified Pius's bull by allowing English Romanists to obey
and accept Elizabeth as queen "*rebus sic stantibus.*" But, of course, the
implication is that when the rebellion came, Roman Catholics in England were to be released from oaths of loyalty and participate in the rebellion against the queen's government.

But the homily states emphatically that subjects are no more qualified to judge the merits of their king than the foot is qualified to judge
the head: the result could only be rebellion. And rebellion is the greatest
of all mischiefs. Moreover, a rebel is worse than the worst prince, and
rebellion is far worse than the worst government of the worst prince. Just
as Bale had cited scriptural texts to indicate examples of good men who

---

[15]Irving Ribner cites other Tudor documents in which this doctrine of absolutism appears: John Cheke's *The hurt of sedicion howe grevous it is to a communwelth* (1549, repeated in Holinshed in 1587), an Edwardian homily entitled *An Exhortation concerning
good order and obedience to Rulers and Magistrates*, John Jewel's *Apologia Ecclesiae Anglicanae* (1562, 1564, 1581, 1591), John Whitgift's *Defence of the Answer to the Admonition
Against the Reply of Thomas Cartwright*, Richard Hooker's *Of the Laws of Ecclesiastical
Polity*, and Thomas Bilson's *True Difference Between Christian Subjection and Unchristian
Rebellion* (1585). *The English History Play in the Age of Shakespeare* (Princeton: Princeton
University Press, 1957) 311-12.

obeyed bad kings, the homily recites examples of those who obeyed wicked rulers, even when it meant great personal discomfort: for example, the Virgin, in advanced pregnancy, obeyed a decree of Caesar Augustus to submit to an official census. Indeed, says the homilist, rebellion represents a combination of all the sins against God and humanity.

Curiously, in the play John's subjects do not seem to rebel against him because of the cardinal's injunction. Shakespeare suggests rather that there are other motives more immediate than the pope's deposition. For example, Englishmen at large are in a state of unrest because they believe that King John is responsible for Prince Arthur's death. Hubert de Burgh relates to John the strange goings-on in the city and the widespread rumors circulating among the commoners: "Young Arthur's death is common in their mouths" (4.2.187). Even when the nobles are about to rebel against their king, it is not because of any religious dispute; it is because their king has abandoned what great princes must safeguard—magnanimity. Salisbury reflects the rumor concerning Arthur's death: "It is apparent foul play, and 'tis shame / That greatness should so grossly offer it" (4.2.93-94). It is after the nobles have discovered Arthur's dead body that Salisbury justifies his decision to rebel against his king upon the basis of John's wickedness.

> The King hath dispossessed himself of us.
> We will not line his thin bestainéd cloak
> With our pure honors, nor attend the foot
> That leaves the print of blood where'er it walks.   (4.3.23-26)

By the time rebellion breaks out in earnest, King John has submitted to Rome and acknowledged England as a papal fief. But even before the king's submission, Pembroke implies that Pandulph's deposition did not alter John's status as England's king.

> This "once again," but that your Highness pleased,
> Was once superfluous. You were crowned before,
> That that high royalty was ne'er plucked off,
> The faiths of men ne'er stainéd with revolt.
> Fresh expectation troubled not the land
> With any longed-for change or better state.   (4.2.3-8)

Indeed, it is not a question of rebellion caused by the pope's demands, but of rebellion that occurs against a king who apparently has proven himself an evil ruler by "murdering" Arthur.

While the commoners and nobles may seem to have just cause for rebellion against their king, Shakespeare continues to deal with the question by demonstrating the truth expressed in the homily "Against Disobedience and Wilful Rebellion." That is, rebellion is worse than the worst government of the worst prince. Salisbury, expressing the outrage of the "distempered lords," not only determines to cease obeying his king, but he also dedicates himself to vengeance.

> It is the shameful work of Hubert's hand,
> The practice and the purpose of the King;
> From whose obedience I forbid my soul,
> Kneeling before this ruin of sweet life,
> And breathing to his breathless excellence
> The incense of a vow, a holy vow,
> Never to taste the pleasures of the world,
> Never to be infected with delight
> Nor conversant with ease and idleness
> Till I have set a glory to this hand
> By giving it the worship of revenge.   (4.3.62-72)

The practical consequence of rebellion in the realm is the invasion by the French. To Shakespeare's highly patriotic and freedom-loving audience, nothing could have been more detestable, except perhaps a similar invasion by the Spanish. One can imagine the effect upon the audience hearing the Bastard's account of French successes.

> All Kent hath yielded. Nothing there holds out
> But Dover Castle. London hath received,
> Like a kind host, the Dauphin and his powers.
> Your nobles will not hear you, but are gone
> To offer service to your enemy,
> And wild amazement hurries up and down
> The little number of your doubtful friends.   (5.1.30-36)

John submits to Rome only because he seeks to avoid the bloodshed of his subjects. Yet as he submits, the Bastard reflects a thoroughly English spirit of Elizabethan patriotism in his response to the news of John's new peace with the papacy.

> Oh, inglorious league!
> Shall we, upon the footing of our land,

Send fair-play orders and make compromise,
Insinuation, parley, and base truce
To arms invasive?   (5.1.65-69)

It is almost too late when the rebels discover what a dear price England must pay for rebellion. With the Dauphin installed in London and refusing to cease hostilities, even after the pretext of invasion has been removed, the rebels realize, perhaps for the first time, that foreign domination by a greedy French prince will be the consequence of their own disloyalty and rebellion.

In such a case, rebellion proved to be worse than any alleged evil on the king's part. The rebels have committed an unnatural sin against God's laws in taking up arms against their anointed king and in betraying England to a foreign prince. Shakespeare underscores this point by assigning to the Bastard—here the voice of English nationalism—the most celebrated lines of the play.

This England never did, nor never shall,
Lie at the proud foot of a conqueror
But when it first did help to wound itself.
Now these her princes are come home again,
Come the three corners of the world in arms,
And we shall shock them. Naught shall make us rue
If England to itself do rest but true.[16]   (5.7.112-118)

Shakespeare's audience, if not convinced before, could hardly avoid a proper response to the question of justifiable rebellion, even in the case of a wicked king who may be an enemy of the Church. It is certainly possible that Shakespeare may have had English Roman Catholics in mind when he raised the question, since Cardinal Allen and the papacy assumed that Roman Catholics would rise up in armed rebellion when the anticipated foreign invasion of England began.

---

[16]Compare the following passage from Holinshed's account of Campion's trial (1581): "This little Lland, God hauing so bountifullie bestowed his blessings vpon it, that except it prooue false within it selfe, no treason whatsoeuer can preuaile against it, and the pope being hereof verie well persuaded, by reason that all his attempts haue prooued of no effect: he hath found out a meane, whereby he assureth himselfe to speed of his desire. Secret rebellion must be stirred here at home among our selues, the harts of the people must be obdurated against God and their prince: so that *when a foren power shall on a sudden inuade this realme, the subjects thus seduced most ioine with these in armes,* & so shall the pope atteine the sum of his wish." 4:449. (Italics mine.)

A fourth question raised by Shakespeare's play would have been timely while bringing into focus the case of John's submission to Rome and a clear example of Rome's policy with dissenting nations: Do foreign princes have the right to interfere with a king's administration of his own dominions?

The answer would have been easy for the highly nationalistic English of Shakespeare's day. But such an answer would have presupposed the whole controversy with the papacy reaching back to the days of William the Conqueror. William's case was well known: he was willing to accept the pope's spiritual jurisdiction, but he would not acknowledge Rome's temporal claims within his dominions. William insisted, successfully, upon the ancient right of English kings to appoint their own bishops (lay investiture). Yet when the German Henry insisted upon similar claims, Pope Hildebrand deposed him and forced his submission in the snow of Canossa. By acting as both governor of the Church in England and Defender of the Faith, William the Conqueror limited papal jurisdiction in England.

By the time Shakespeare's play was composed, the temporal claims of the papacy had increased to the point that loyal Roman Catholics could acknowledge as their sovereigns only those whom the papacy permitted. The right of a prince to rule in his dominions was dependent upon a prerequisite of obedience and loyalty to the Holy See. If a sovereign defected from such obedience, or if he succeeded to the throne without papal consent, the pope could depose him as a heretic and call upon loyal Catholic countries to effect the deposition.

On the other hand, throughout the Middle Ages England had maintained that while her kings owed spiritual fealty to Rome, the papacy had no right to interfere with the temporal administration of matters claimed by royal prerogatives from the time of Edward the Confessor. By the time of the English Reformation, the changed conception of papal jurisdiction could be regarded by England only as papal usurpation.

In the play, act 1 proposes a war between France and England on the pretext that John is a usurper. Consequently, France claims the right to invade England, if necessary, since John's usurpation "religiously provokes" such recourse. But Shakespeare makes it clear that France's real motive is more one of personal gain than religious provocation. As Philip confesses, France came to champion the widow Constance's claims for Arthur, but dropped the cause in favor of personal advantage and greed:

" . . . In her right we came; / Which we, God knows, have turned another way / To our own vantage" (2.1.548-550).

The Bastard exemplifies the perceptive English subject as he comments upon France's apparent duplicity, "fickle France," and he rightly sees that commodity is the real motivating factor in France's enterprise. In act 3, Cardinal Pandulph almost parallels instances of papal policy by urging Prince Lewis to invade England.

> The bastard Faulconbridge
> Is now in England, ransacking the Church,
> Offending charity. If but a dozen French
> Were there in arms, there would be as a call
> To train ten thousand English to their side,
> Or as a little snow, tumbled about,
> Anon becomes a mountain. O noble Dauphin,
> Go with me to the King. 'Tis wonderful
> What may be wrought out of their discontent
> Now that their souls are topful of offense.   (3.4.171-180)

But while Lewis agrees to invade England upon a religious pretext, Cardinal Pandulph appeals to Lewis's covetousness to enlist his aid in the papal enterprise. He tells the prince that when Arthur is dead, Lewis becomes heir to Arthur's claims because of his recent marriage to Lady Blanch: "You, in the right of Lady Blanch, your wife, / May then make all the claim that Arthur did" (3.4.142-143). Lewis, taken in by the cardinal's Machiavellian policy, agrees to invade England and says significantly, "Strong reasons make strong actions" (3.4.183).

Shakepeare makes it clear that Lewis's invasion of England, though under the pretext of restoring the realm to papal control, was actually motivated by personal gain. When Lewis sees the cardinal approaching his camp at St. Edmundsbury, he tells the English rebels of his holy enterprise.

> Look, where the holy legate comes apace
> To give us warrant from the hand of Heaven
> And on our actions set the name of right
> With holy breath.   (5.2.65-68)

But even before the cardinal arrives, the Dauphin assures his English rebels that they will share with him in the spoils of victory.

Come, come; for thou shalt thrust thy hand as deep
Into the purse of rich prosperity
As Lewis himself. So, nobles, shall you all
That knit your sinews to the strength of mine.   (5.2.60-63)

When Cardinal Pandulph comes onstage he tells the Dauphin that
since King John has submitted to Rome there is no further need for war;
consequently, Lewis should withdraw from England. Yet, and this is the
crux, Lewis reveals that he has no intention of being ordered about by
the cardinal.

Your Grace shall pardon me, I will not back.
I am too high-born to be propertied,
To be a secondary at control,
Or useful servingman and instrument
To any sovereign state throughout the world.   (5.2.78-82)

He also accuses Pandulph of being the instigator of the whole business.

Your breath first kindled the dead coal of wars
Between this chastised kingdom and myself
And brought in matter that should feed this fire;
And now 'tis far too huge to be blown out
With that same weak wind which enkindled it.
You taught me to know the face of right,
Acquainted me with interest to this land,
Yea, thrust this enterprise into my heart.   (5.2.83-90)

Then the Dauphin lowers the shield of hypocrisy upon which he had
justified his invasion of England and reveals his true motivation.

And come ye now to tell me John hath made
His peace with Rome? What is that peace to me?
I, by the honor of my marriage bed,
After young Arthur, claim this land for mine;
And, now it is half-conquered, must I back
Because that John hath made his peace with Rome?
Am I Rome's slave?   (5.2.91-97)

Thus fired by his own covetousness, Lewis assumes a position not
unlike that taken by John at the beginning of the play in his attitude toward Rome. Shakespeare demonstrates that Lewis's sense of holy mission is merely a pretext for invading England in his own right. When the
papal legate tries to stop him, Lewis defies the legate and refuses to be
ruled by Rome.

The parallel to Spanish Philip's pretext for the Armada is too apparent at this point to be ignored. While Philip claimed to be the champion of the papacy in restoring "heretical" nations to the Roman See, in the case of his invasion of England his motivation was that of pressing his claim to the English throne. He claimed the right of succession in England on three grounds: (1) his previous marriage to Mary Tudor, (2) his inheritance of the English throne from Mary Stuart's will, and (3) his descent from John of Gaunt. Shakespeare's play implies that foreign invasions of England in the name of the Holy Church are in reality no more than the personal ambitions of greedy princes. It is certainly true in the case of the Dauphin.

If Shakespeare's audience felt a sense of betrayal because of John's submission to Rome while foreign powers plundered the realm, it would have felt a pleasant relief when the Bastard announces that King John was not entirely serious about the whole business. The king has not submitted to Pandulph as thoroughly as it may have seemed.

> For at hand,
> Not trusting to this halting legate here,
> Whom he hath used rather for sport than need,
> Is warlike John; and in his forehead sits
> A bare-ribbed Death, whose office is this day
> To feast upon whole thousands of the French.   (5.2.173-178)

During the last battle, the rebellious English nobles return to John's camp, the Dauphin's armada is wrecked on Goodwin Sands, and King John himself is maliciously poisoned by a monk at Swinstead Abbey. Yet it is a victory for England, and the French forces are compelled to withdraw. Future hope for England becomes apparent in the magnanimous spirit of the king's son, Prince Henry.

Shakespeare's play supports the general Elizabethan consensus that all such efforts on the part of foreign powers to invade England were without legal and moral justification. They were, in fact, no more than instances of usurpation—whether they were initiated by the papacy or by covetous princes. King John's early response to King Philip's interference may very well reflect the attitude of Englishmen in this regard: "Alack, thou dost usurp authority" (2.1.118). It is, therefore, essential to understand the technical aspects of the political-religious point of view before one can appreciate how skillfully Shakespeare has managed the question he raises. His attitude in the play is thoroughly Protestant insofar as he denies the papacy any right to invade by force the dominions of a reigning Christian prince. Shakespeare also seems to vindicate the Protestant assumption that since kings rule as anointed ministers of God, they are not answerable to any foreign power, temporal or spiritual. No foreign princes have the right to interfere with a Christian king's administration of his own dominions.

In *King John* Shakespeare has used the highly charged materials of ecclesiastical controversy for their artistic value. By reducing the controversy to basic political questions and lifting them above the contemporary strife to an earlier, more remote period of English history, he is able to maintain a degree of objectivity missing in the writings of other dramatists who had used similar materials.

While Shakespeare does not seem to be a violent partisan of the Settlement position, one cannot avoid observing that he comes through as a wise and perceptive spokesman for his age. For example, while the traditional commentaries relegate to Shakespeare an uncommon tolerance for Roman Catholics and the Old Faith, it is difficult to ignore the fact that he has made of Cardinal Pandulph a character much darker than necessary—almost the Vice of the play. A careful study of the cardinal shows him to be the cause of discord and strife among nations. He is the instigator of rebellion, he demands that King Philip break his sacred vows of peace and friendship with England, he appeals to the Dauphin through dubious means to invade England, and he seems to serve all the while at the altar of Commodity. Lewis made these exact charges against the legate, and the cardinal himself confessed that he alone was responsible for the rebellion in England and the foreign invasion.

> It was my breath that blew this tempest up,
> Upon your stubborn usage of the Pope;
> But since you are a gentle convertite,
> My tongue shall hush again this storm of war
> And make fair weather in your blustering land.   (5.1.17-21)

But, of course, not even the papal legate could restrain the forces of discord he had released. If one persists in the contention that Shakespeare was always fair in dramatizing the Old Faith, it is indeed difficult to explain his treatment of the cardinal.

What is nevertheless gratifying about Shakespeare's use of religious controversy in *King John* is that he universalizes the conflict on a purely human basis. Pandulph may function as a papal legate in the play, but at the same time he is a fallible human being, subject to invoking unworthy policy for what he considers a worthy end. By the same token, John may be a Christian prince, but he is also subject to the same disintegrating forces that enter into the experience of all mortals: he is covetous, often ignoble, and Machiavellian in policy, but he is no villain. When his land is torn apart by hostile armies, he submits to the pontiff to spare his subjects further bloodshed. King Philip leads his armies against England in the name of justice for Prince Arthur, but he is vulnerable to Commodity and soon forgets his worthy commission. The Dauphin invades England on behalf of Cardinal Pandulph, but he too serves Commodity.

The issues, therefore, are never a simple matter with Roman Catholics as Vices and Protestants as Virtues. Rather, each character pursues his own course through the drama as a fallible human being. Perhaps it is such an awareness of human character as this that separates Shakespeare from other Tudor dramatists.

CONCLUSION

The appearance of the historical controversy between English kings and Roman popes in various official documents helps explain the English fear of foreign domination at any level, and it helps provide a frame of reference in which many plays of the Tudor period were composed. Dramatists reflected the natural fears, suspicions, and attitudes of the audiences for whom they wrote. The attitude pervasive in Tudor drama was the notion that Rome had gained control of the Church in England by usurpation.

Much of the drama results in propaganda against an ecclesiastical polity traditionally hostile to the English temperament. If there is a unifying theme running through related historical documents of the Middle Ages, it probably is one that shows England heroically attempting to recover ancient royal prerogatives in ecclesiastical affairs as she knew them in the days of Edward the Confessor, before Roman pontiffs usurped those prerogatives by "innovation."

As Tudor apologists saw it, England's struggle with the papacy was never a matter limited to Henry's reformation of the Church in England, or even limited to the sixteenth century; it was a recurring controversy from the eleventh century onward. For this reason, the materials of religious history provided dramatists with a valuable source of dramatic possibilities. The playwright, by the very nature of his art, must discover conflict which will at once be relevant and interesting.

One of the most important conflicts is religious conflict. It has always been of great concern to humanity in its progress through the ages.

Whenever Tudor playwrights used religious conflict in stage plays, it
generally appeared as a direct appeal to the audience in the guise of apologetics, propaganda, and later entertainment. Tudor dramatists recognized in the religious controversy taking place during their lifetimes one
of the most relevant issues for their audiences, and they used materials
of the controversy with varying degrees of success for dramatic effect.

Reformation interludes composed during the polemical period ex-
ploit themes of ecclesiastical corruption, but with a deliberate attempt to
show a direct relationship between the Old Faith and moral decadence,
particularly among the clergy. Stage plays supporting the Reformation
often suggest a rationale to justify official endeavors to purify the Church
in England by expelling papal innovation unauthorized by Scripture and
contrary to apostolic Christianity.

The most significant polemical dramatist supporting the early English Reformation is John Bale, whose *King John* seems to be the per-
sonification of Henry VIII and his controversy with the papacy over
matters of temporal jurisdiction. Indeed, *King John* seems to depend
upon various statutes of Henry's Reformation Parliament before 1538 for
its effect as an apologetic. By following the Tudor habit of reading contemporary history into earlier centuries, Bale manages to present King
John as a proto-Reformer of the Church in England—a patriot king who
defied the pope's policy of usurpation of royal prerogatives.

Yet, Bale's thesis is identical to the Tudor understanding of divine
right: a king rules in his dominions as the minister of God, both for good
and evil, without permission from Rome. As such, a king's subjects owe
to him prime allegiance, loyalty, and obedience, which even the pope
cannot lawfully forbid. To deny fidelity to an anointed king is tantamount to breaking the laws of God—regardless of Rome's interference.
Since, according to Bale, the pope is really a man like other men, his
"inter-meddling" with the natural expectations of a king from his subjects must be discounted as an instance of usurpation. In all cases, "We
should obey God rather than men," and the pope is just a man like other
men.

Bale's *King John* provides a rationale for the Reformation on a popular level. The whole play exposes a corrupt ecclesiastical system prop-
agated by "popish" innovation and characterized by usurpation,
tyranny, hypocrisy, fraud, greed, and murder. John, however, is the
spirit of the English Reformation as he attempts, almost single-hand-

edly, a premature struggle against the dark forces of the Antichrist and a corrupt clergy. The play itself is an *exemplum* of what happens whenever English subjects obey a "foreign potentate" rather than the pure Word of God and His anointed. Yet, while the play serves the cause of polemics, it also contains many effective dramatic elements which would have appealed to a Reformation audience in 1538. Even more remarkable is the fact that Bale constructed a lengthy play almost entirely out of the heated issues of ecclesiastical controversy being enacted during the decade in which his play was written. The work, in fact, becomes a Protestant tract supporting official documents of the early Reformation in England.

Generally speaking, the polemical drama serves the cause of propaganda more than art. Such plays possess dramatic possibilities, vivid scenes, and conflict; however, the playwrights lack restraint and Shakespeare's sense of universality. Instead they seem to serve causes more immediate than producing enduring works of art. Yet, when one examines the contemporary scene, it is understandable that great drama may have been practically impossible when such controversial elements were used, because the dramatists were too close to the turbulent events to gain clear focus and objectivity.

Stage plays written after the Elizabethan Settlement reveal a more effective use of ecclesiastical controversy as material for art. Although much of the old hostility against Roman Catholicism remained throughout the Elizabethan period, most of the derogatory allusions were prompted by the continuing fear of foreign invasions from loyal Catholic powers on the Continent. Consequently, much antipapal propaganda continues to come through the drama, though this is no longer the central point of focus, except in rare instances such as Dekker's *Whore of Babylon*.

The Elizabethan Settlement was the century's most decisive event in the religious controversy. It established the Protestant theory in England to the satisfaction of a nation horrified at the thought of Bloody Mary's persecution of "heretics" in the name of the Holy Church. Moreover, following the Elizabethan Settlement, the machinations of Rome to reclaim the Church of England for the Roman Curia provided dramatists with a valuable source for lively humor, intrigue, espionage, mystery, and quips at the common foe—none of which would have been lost on an Elizabethan audience.

Academic drama in such pieces as *Gammer Gurtons Nedle* and *Misogonus* present the ecclesiastic in the literary tradition of the Sir John type, brought down from the Middle Ages. But here he is the ignorant, depraved, and worldly stereotype of the Roman Catholic cleric who is more interested in his ale house revelries than in his ecclesiastical duties. The depraved cleric, while not the center of attention, becomes the agent through which dramatists effectively satirize certain doctrines, practices, and ceremonies of the Old Faith. He is still a Vice, but he is now more mischievous than malicious.

The controversial materials are too skillfully handled in most of the Academic plays to detract from the deliberate and lively, if sometimes ribald, humor. In the Academic drama one sees that the Protestant bias always lies beneath the surface humor by associating Roman Catholic clerics, doctrines, and devotional works with ignorance, medievalism, superstition, and religious practices currently out of vogue at Court. Yet, if one could momentarily disregard the Elizabethan animus towards the Old Faith, the Academic drama can be seen as having a close kinship in technique with the clever interludes of John Heywood, although themes other than clerical corruption are apparent, and the cleric is more of the side issue than the central focus of attention in the Academic plays.

On the other hand, *Conflict of Conscience*, a representative Elizabethan interlude, is a Protestant *exemplum* supporting the Settlement point of view against Roman Catholic Machiavellian policy. Moreover, while it contains all the bitterness of the polemical period, it is more akin to pulpit drama than to the more dramatically effective genres developing collaterally. It becomes a Protestant tract directed against recent decisions of the Council of Trent, although the prologue announces that its purpose is to teach a moral lesson and stir up the audience to "godliness." It is, in fact, violently antipapal, and it attempts to gain popular acceptance by using Morality play devices and by appealing to an antipapal audience. With Mary Tudor's Smithfield fires still burning in the consciousness of the nation, the theme of Catholic persecution seems to be exploited for its emotional effect rather than for the dramatic possibility such a theme affords.

Yet, *Conflict of Conscience* is unique in that while it possesses all the elements for great drama, the playwright possesses no sense of the dramatic possibilities of his materials. The result is an inferior play, tedious and artificial. The preacher submerges the artist and only the polemics come through effectively. However, the carefully constructed arguments favoring the Settlement position of the Church of England at the expense of Roman Catholicism are as good as most of the polemical tracts and official propaganda of the times.

During the exciting decade that gave enduring fame to the University Wits, the history of drama seems to have been revolutionized. Certain of the Wits had learned in their experimentation that the materials of ecclesiastical controversy must not, as in the case of *Conflict of Conscience*, occupy unwarranted attention as the central focus of their art—unless, of course, they were reduced to a political principal such as the legal or moral right of any foreign power to usurp the prerogatives of a sovereign king in his own dominions.

Peele's *Old Wives' Tale* employs controversial elements only incidentally to satirize the Old Faith and its "superstition." The animus becomes political rather than religious as it provides a mild thrust at Spain—the temporal arm of the papacy—whose Armada had secured a place of undying infamy in the Elizabethan consciousness. Yet, the controversial elements are rather more a concession to an audience hostile to Spain and fearful of another invasion. There are no polemics, little propaganda, and no vitriolic denunciations of the papacy. In this case, the subtle allusions to the Old Faith do not call attention away from the work of art.

Greene's *Friar Bacon and Friar Bungay* seems innocuous enough on the surface as good entertainment for a popular audience. However, by studying references to Elizabethan attitudes toward ecclesiastical practices, particularly to the Royal Injunctions, one can see that Greene reduces the Old Faith to so much "sorcery" by associating the work of the friars with demonic powers. Moreover, by his concession to contemporary attitudes he "exposes" the whole monastic institution. Although Greene uses Roman Catholic trappings and practices to create atmosphere, they are harmless items in themselves, for there are no polemics and the elements of ecclesiastical controversy are not obtrusive. On the other hand, an anti-Catholic audience could not fail to make the necessary association of the Old Faith with medieval superstition, ignorance, and superficial piety, even though the drama as a whole is not disparaging of the Roman Catholic faith.

Marlowe's *Jew of Malta*, however, is often more obviously anti-Catholic than plays by Peele and Greene. The drama as a whole seems to be an exposé on several levels of Machiavellian policy which Roman Catholic clerics openly denounce but secretly employ in their ambitious climb to Peter's chair. Marlowe exploits contemporary Elizabethan attitudes toward licentious nuns and friars for comic effect. At the same time, he "exposes" auricular confession and the rascality of friars. Yet, Marlowe's use of the depraved clerics and their Machiavellian policy provides effective comic relief for his tragedy. As such, the indecorous employment of friars is little more than their conventional depiction as lecherous, depraved, greedy, and unscrupulous ecclesiastics. But for an Elizabethan audience, the comical treatment of ecclesiastics of the Old Faith could never be merely for entertainment as it had been in the pre-Reformation drama of John Heywood.

Viewed together, the three Wits use controversial materials without polemical intent, although the old hostility is always beneath the surface humor, functioning as a bias for the antipapal audience. Their use of satire is generally mild and innocuous, for they had learned to subordinate the controversial elements to create atmosphere, to enhance the dramatic situation, and to provide an aid for convincing imitation.

It remained, however, for Shakespeare to use the ecclesiastical controversy in such a way that his personal attitudes are so unclear they are still subject to debate. In *King John*, Shakespeare reflects the Anglican viewpoint of his Settlement audience, although he had learned, no doubt from the bold experiments of the University Wits, to use the controversial elements for their dramatic value rather than as an occasion for Reformation polemics.

Yet, because of the very controversial nature of the historical circumstances surrounding King John, Shakespeare nowhere better demonstrates his genius as an enduring artist than in reducing the whole conflict with the papacy to a matter of politics and avoiding many individual grievances of Protestants against Catholics. A careful examination of those political principles as they are reflected in the drama and current events during Elizabeth's controversy with Rome would suggest that Shakespeare echoes commonplace attitudes and that his response to the principles which he implies reach back in English history at least to the days of William the Conqueror's dispute with Pope Gregory. Shakespeare seems to confirm the belief that the papacy has no legal or scriptural authority to depose kings or to interfere otherwise in their dominions.

Such a skillful handling of the heated issues in the last decade of Rome's persistent endeavor to reclaim England is a tribute to Shakespeare's artistic genius, for so much have the controversial elements become subordinated to his art in *King John* that the play requires a study such as this one to point out the controversial materials that were commonplace to Shakespeare's audience. The fact that the political principles remain long after the theological disputes have been relegated to a place of insignificance by modern readers indicates how skillfully Shakespeare lifted the whole controversy above the bitterness of that century and created a universal issue which is as relevant in the twentieth century as it was in the sixteenth. Instead of following the assumptions of his predecessors, he reduced the absolute rightness and wrongness of the entire ecclesiastical controversy to a matter of political or personal motivation on the part of fallible men in a fallen world. Indeed, when one comes to Shakespeare's treatment of religious controversy in *King John*, one can well agree that the issues as Shakespeare sees them are not restricted for an age; rather, they are relevant for all time.

In a very real sense, religious controversy, while functioning as a source of humor, pathos, setting, and conflict in Tudor drama, is in reality no more than a limited aspect of what has been a vital part of some of the world's great drama from the beginning. Elements of religious conflict are inherent in the history of drama. Some Greek plays, for example, localize the religious conflict as a vain struggle by mortals against the inevitable will of the gods. Sometimes, as in the case of Sophocles' *Antigone*, the dramatic conflict is dependent upon a moral choice between divine law and temporal authority. Antigone's dilemma may be one of the earliest expressions of the kind of conflict pervasive in Tudor plays: Is it better to obey God rather than humans? Wherein lies one's duty when there is a conflict of conscience between divine law and loyalty to the powers that be? Moreover, the dramatic conflict in all such plays is enhanced by the knowledge that suffering is inevitable in either choice.

Religious conflict in drama still continues to provide one of the most fruitful sources for dramatic conflict. One could examine Tennessee Williams's *Night of the Iguana*, for example, and discover a mingling of elements in the defrocked priest that effect the same essential functions of clerics in Tudor plays: humor, pathos, conflict, and enigmatic characterization. Or one could find in Arthur Miller's *The Crucible* a play composed almost entirely of religious conflict in which John Proctor discovers the impossibility of preserving a measure of loyalty to truth in compromising with temporal-ecclesiastical authority. In this instance, as in the case of Antigone, Proctor sacrifices himself for a principle of truth beyond temporal jurisdiction.

Peter Shaffer's *The Royal Hunt of the Sun* is another example of drama largely dependent upon religious conflict for success. The time of action, curiously enough, takes place between the years 1529 and 1533—the period of Henry VIII's breach with Roman Catholicism. While the controversy between Protestants and Catholics does not enter into the drama, many of the principles that Protestants cited against Roman Catholics during the Reformation become universal on the broad plain of humanitarianism. Pizarro's perceptive analysis of those who destroyed the magnificent Inca civilization in Peru in the name of Christ could easily be a commentary upon any closed system that denies the right of individual religious beliefs.

> Dungballs to all churches that are or ever could be! How I hate you. "Kill who I bid you kill and I will pardon it." . . . How dare you priests bless any man who goes slicing into battle? But no. You slice with him. "Rip!" you scream, "Tear! blind! in the name of Christ!" Tell me soft Father, if Christ was here now, do you think he would kill my Inca?[1]

Indeed, some of the lines could almost come from a Tudor play in the self-revelation of characters blinded by a single-minded adherence to Church dogma. At one point in the conflict, Valverde, a Dominican, tells Pizarro, "No promise to a pagan need bind a Christian."[2] At another place, Atahuallpa, the Inca sovereign, almost reiterates the Protestant grievance against militant Roman Catholic policy when the two priests attempt to convert him. The essence of that exchange follows.

DE NIZZA.   And when he went he left the Pope as Regent
                for him.
VALVERDE.   He has commanded our King to bring all men
                to belief in the true God.

....

[1]Peter Shaffer, *The Royal Hunt of the Sun* (New York: Stein and Day, 1965) 70.

[2]Shaffer, 70.

VALVERDE. (*Together*) In Christ's name
DE NIZZA. therefore I charge you: yield yourself his
    willing vassal.
ATAHUALLPA. I am the vassal of no man. . . .
    Your King is great. . . . But your Pope is mad.
    He gives away countries that are not his.
    His faith also is mad.[3]

Pizarro, thoroughly disgusted by the ecclesiastical bloodthirst of his priests, indites the illogical injustice of the whole ecclesiastical system.

So there is Christian charity. To save my own
    soul I must kill another man!
. . . .
Hail to you, sole judge of love! No salvation
    outside your church: and no love neither. Oh,
    you arrogance! . . . [4]

Father Valverde's reply could easily have been written by a Tudor polemicist: "I'll give you death. When I get back to Spain, a commission will hale you to the stake for what you have said today."[5]

But, of course, this is not Tudor drama, and Shaffer is not derogating Roman Catholicism in favor of Protestantism; rather, he is questioning the universal morality of imposing by compulsion the "God of Europe with all its death and blooding" upon any people. What troubles him, as he tells us, is the fact that man "canalises the greatness of his spiritual awareness into the second-rate formula of a Church—any Church" and "puts into the hands of other men the reins of repression and the whip of Sole Interpretation."[6]

One can assume that since mankind's religious conflict has provided an integral part throughout the history of drama to the present day, it will continue to provide playwrights with a powerful and appealing focus of attention as long as man believes in the validity of religious experience. If drama is really an imitation of life, religious conflict—whether it be

---

[3]Shaffer, 37.

[4]Shaffer, 71.

[5]Shaffer, 72.

[6]Shaffer, vii.

the ecclesiastical controversy of the sixteenth century or the search for extra-temporal awareness in the twentieth—will supply the materials for universal themes in the dramatization of Everyman.

INDEX

MUP *Tudor Drama and Religious Controversy*

Binding designed by Alesa Jones and Margaret Jordan Brown

Interior typography design by Margaret Jordan Brown

Composition by MUP Composition Department

Production specifications:
    text paper—60 pound Warren's Olde Style
    endpapers—Multicolor Antique Thistle
    cover—(on .088 boards) Spine Joanna Eton #10500 (gray) Front and Back
    Cover Joanna Eton # 19990 (black)

Printing (offset lithography) by Omnipress of Macon, Inc., Macon, Georgia

Binding by John H. Dekker and Sons, Inc., Grand Rapids, Michigan